KICK OFF
The F.A. Carling Premiership
TRAVEL GUIDE 1995/6

First published in 1995
by Sidan Press
40 Harrowby Street
London W1H 5HX.

Copyright 1995 © Sidan Press
All rights reserved.

NO PART OF THIS PUBLICATION MAY BE REPRODUCED, STORED IN A RETRIEVAL SYSTEM, OR TRANSMITTED IN ANY FORM OR BY ANY MEANS, ELECTRONIC, MECHANICAL, PHOTOCOPYING OR OTHERWISE, WITHOUT THE PRIOR WRITTEN PERMISSION OF THE PUBLISHER.

Reprographics by GraphiService,
London W1H 5HR.
Printing by KNP Group Limited,
Redditch B98 0RE.

ISBN No. 0 9526041 0 8

British Library Cataloguing in Publication Data:
A catalogue record for *Kick Off* is available
from the British Library.

Every effort has been made to ensure that the information given in this guide is as accurate and up-to-date as possible at the time of going to press. Details do change, however, and the publisher cannot accept responsibility for any consequences arising from the use of this book. If you come across an incorrect detail that we could amend for next year, please let us know.

KICK OFF

The F.A. Carling Premiership

TRAVEL GUIDE 1995/6

SIDAN ❦ PRESS
PREMIER SPORTS PUBLICATIONS
40 HARROWBY STREET LONDON W1H 5HX

KICK OFF

THE F.A. CARLING PREMIERSH[IP] TRAVEL GUIDE

CONTENTS
Foreword by Rick Parry
Euro '96
95/96 Fixtures
ARSENAL
ASTON VILLA
BLACKBURN ROVERS
BOLTON WANDERERS
CHELSEA
COVENTRY CITY
EVERTON
LEEDS UNITED
LIVERPOOL
MANCHESTER CITY
MANCHESTER UNITED
MIDDLESBROUGH
NEWCASTLE UNITED
NOTTINGHAM FOREST
QUEENS PARK RANGERS
SHEFFIELD WEDNESDAY
SOUTHAMPTON
TOTTENHAM HOTSPUR
WEST HAM UNITED
WIMBLEDON
WEMBLEY STADIUM
Mileage Chart

Welcome to the first official travel guide to England's twenty Premier League football clubs. Here you will find everything you need to know to get to a game: ticket prices, telephone numbers, travel routes and maps, plus suggestions for where to eat, where to stay, and what to check out in the area if you are making a trip of it. The Premier League continues to go from strength to strength each year, and this season promises to be full of outstanding moments and glory. We hope you will find KICK OFF accurate and useful and easy to use, and we wish you an exciting season around the greatest football pitches of this land.

USING THE MAPS
The maps are designed to provide a clear route from all points to the stadium. They are figurative only and not to scale. The nearest or most convenient motorway or A-road is indicated on the outside band in red. This shows the most likely point of approach. In the mid-section of the map, routes are given which are direct and suitable for newcomers to the area, and which, where relevant, lead to parking areas. Wherever possible, roads run in the direction and attitude that one would find when driving, and left and right turns are given accurately. We have also tried to provide a simple road grid in the vicinity of the stadium which would allow a person taking a wrong turn to find their way again. Inevitably, some sections are shortened and others shaped to fit the format. The roads near the stadium shown in blue are within approximately fifteen-minutes walking distance of the ground.

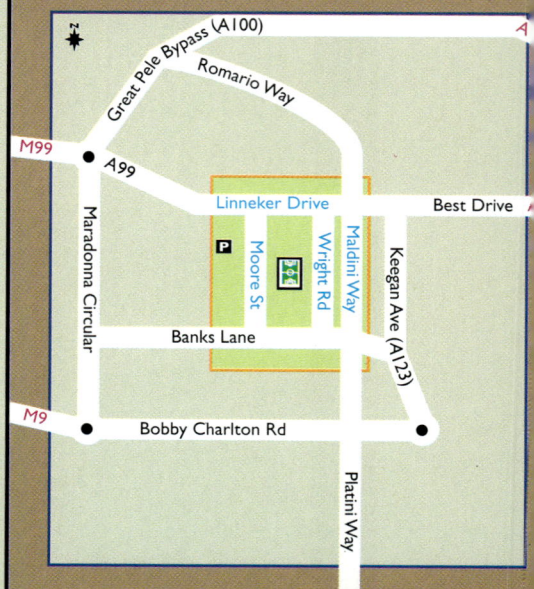

A FOREWORD BY JONATHAN NYE
NATIONAL SPONSORSHIP MANAGER, BASS BREWERS

This season Carling begins its third season as proud sponsors of what we feel is the world's greatest football club competition. It is as far as we are concerned a sponsorship that means far more than simply the race to be Carling Premiership champions.

It is just as much about the pride and passion of fans as it is about the skill and action on the pitch. Supporters give football its atmosphere and its drama. And it is perhaps those who travel the thousands of miles every week to support their team away from home who do more than any others to define the true British football fan.

To hear two sets of supporters in full cry in a ground is an experience which is almost entirely unique to British football. In no other football-loving country is the ritual of following your team through thick and thin so fervently acted out as it is here by the thousands of people who nothing of travelling the entire length of the country to cheer their side on. This book will hopefully make some of those journeys easier and more enjoyable.

For our third season as sponsors of the Carling Premiership we are once again planning a comprehensive programme of football-related activities in pubs and clubs. In many Carling stockists you will get the chance to watch live matches on Monday nights and in those and hundreds of others there will be special promotions which will add to your enjoyment of the game we all love. Some of you may also be competing in your own Carling Premiership - the Carling Cup, which is the world's biggest-ever five-a-side competition.

Look out also for the hundreds of ticket competitions that we run in the national press, on national radio and local radio. Every week these give everyone a chance to attend the biggest and best games in the Carling Premiership.

I'd like to wish all supporters a safe journey on your travels and your team a successful season.

Cheers,

Jonathan Nye.

The F.A. Premier League
16 Lancaster Gate
London W2 3LW

Chairman: **Sir John Quinton**
Chief Executive: **Rick Parry**
Secretary: **Mike Foster**
Assistant Secretary: **Adrian Cook**
Sales & Operations Manager: **Richard Carpenter**
Director of Youth: **Dave Richardson**

CHAMPIONS

1992-1993 Manchester United
1993-1994 Manchester United
1994-1995 Blackburn Rovers

Letter from the Chief Executive of the Premier League

We have produced this book to be of assistance to all fans of the Premier League, whether a regular or occasional supporter. We are sure it will be of great use as you travel to and from clubs.

The Premier League is now entering its fourth season and we have come a long way since we started. We have had two very worthy champions with Manchester United lifting the trophy twice and Blackburn Rovers securing the title on the final day of the season. This season looks to be a challenging open field with many clubs having a good chance of the title.

The supporters now have some of the best facilities available, that are continuously being upgraded. Equally important, the quality of football has been excellent and at times outstanding. And with the Premier League now attracting the best foreign players in the world, we have some very exciting times ahead of us. We must not rest on our laurels but continue successful and responsible progress.

I hope every fan has an enjoyable and interesting season.

Rick Parry

FOOTBALL COMES HOME

Every season there is a growing sense of excitement as the Premier and other league titles, together with cup competitions, come to a climax. This season the feeling of anticipation will be greater than ever. Not only will there be all the buzz associated with our domestic competitions, there will also be an increasing sense of awareness that big time international football is about to arrive at our grounds in the form of EURO 96.

The European Football Championship Finals have never taken place in England before. After the Olympics and the World Cup, the European Championship represents the next biggest sporting event in the world. Not since 1966 will English football fans have seen anything like it.

EURO 96 kicks off on Saturday 8th June when England will play at Wembley against opponents yet to be revealed. After that twenty-three more Group games will take place in the space of eleven days. By the time we reach the Final on 30th June there will have been thirty-one top international games in just three weeks.

Apart from Wembley, seven other venues will be used for the Championships. Joining Wembley for Group A games will be Villa Park. Group B will play at Elland Road and St James' Park, Group C will be at Old Trafford and Anfield while Group D will take place at Hillsborough and The City Ground, Nottingham. Once the Group games are over the Quarter-Finals (22nd and 23rd June) will be played at Wembley, Villa Park, Anfield and Old Trafford. The latter, together with Wembley, will then host the Semi-Finals on 26th June.

As our own season starts there are still forty-seven European countries battling it out for a place in EURO 96 in eight different qualifying groups. These games began last September and will not be completed until mid November 1995. The eight group winners will then qualify for the Championship as will the six best second placed teams. England, as the host nation, automatically qualifies while the sixteenth place goes to the winner of a play-off game to be held at Anfield on Wednesday 13th December. This will be between the two remaining second placed teams from the qualifying groups.

Several countries already look well on the way to reaching the Finals but a number of intriguing questions have yet to be answered. Can Scotland add further domestic drama by qualifying in Group eight? Will Croatia finish top of Group four? Will World Cup semi-finalists Sweden still make it after a run of disappointing results? That said, it will be surprising if the established names are not all there. Germany, Italy, Spain, Norway and Portugal are all doing well. There is still a doubt about Holland but many fans in England will be hoping the Netherlands make it if only to provide the possibility of revenge for England's defeat in 1993. Another participant looks likely to be the ever popular Republic of Ireland.

The Final will be played at Wembley.

Just before Christmas (17th December) the Final Draw for EURO 96 will be broadcast live on both BBC and ITV from the International Convention Centre in Birmingham. It will be at this moment when we will know the three teams England must face in their opening games and when we will discover which countries are playing at each of the venues. The scene will be set for the real drama to unfold.

The EURO 96 tournament slogan is "Football Comes Home" and for English fans it will provide a chance in a lifetime opportunity to see international football at its best. It promises to be, in everyway, a festival of football that nobody will want to miss.

THIS YEAR YOUR SEASON'S GUARANTEED TO

END AT WEMBLEY

It's the biggest European Football Championship Finals ever staged and it's in England. Sixteen teams, the best of continental football, contesting one of sport's greatest trophies. The world can only watch, but you can experience it for real.

PHONE NOW ON 0178 274 1996 FOR TICKET DETAILS. TICKET APPLICATION FORMS ARE ALSO AVAILABLE AT ALL BRANCHES OF THE MIDLAND BANK

Football Comes Home TM and EURO 96 TM and its designations are registered trademarks and cannot be used without the express authority of either The Football Association Ltd, UEFA or ISL Marketing AG

F.A. CARLING PREMIERSHIP FIXTURES 1995/96

Home teams listed on the right; Away teams across the top.

Home \ Away	ARSENAL	ASTON VILLA	BLACKBURN	BOLTON	CHELSEA	COVENTRY	EVERTON	LEEDS	LIVERPOOL	MAN CITY	MAN UTD	MIDDLESBRO	NEWCASTLE	NOTTS FOREST	QPR	SHEFF WED	SOUTHAMPTON	TOTTENHAM	WEST HAM	WIMBLEDON
ARSENAL	—	2/12	27/4	30/10	30/9	26/8	23/8	14/10	23/12	10/9	30/3	13/1	2/1	10/2	2/3	8/4	9/12	18/11	24/2	16/3
ASTON VILLA	21/10	—	9/9	10/2	6/4	30/9	26/8	2/3	25/11	13/1	13/4	23/12	23/8	16/3	20/11	4/11	24/2	23/8	4/11	24/2
BLACKBURN	26/11	17/2	—	26/8	4/5	9/12	5/11	1/1	16/9	2/3	30/9	8/11	13/4	13/1	30/9	23/8	6/4	16/3	21/10	23/12
BOLTON	4/5	30/8	3/2	—	22/11	16/3	6/4	2/3	23/9	16/9	20/1	17/2	21/10	20/1	16/12	1/1	25/11	23/12	13/4	19/8
CHELSEA	16/12	14/10	8/4	—	—	28/10	13/1	18/11	16/3	23/12	24/9	26/8	23/8	2/1	30/3	24/2	27/4	11/9	2/3	—
COVENTRY	3/2	20/1	28/10	14/10	30/12	—	9/3	28/10	14/10	23/9	30/12	8/4	19/8	17/2	19/11	4/12	23/3	30/3	26/12	27/4
EVERTON	20/1	28/10	14/10	30/3	23/12	—	—	16/3	18/11	30/8	17/9	16/12	8/4	27/4	3/2	2/12	23/9	1/1
LEEDS	6/4	3/2	23/3	27/12	13/4	4/5	30/12	—	20/1	21/10	9/3	4/11	25/11	22/11	24/2	16/12	30/8	9/9	19/8	23/9
LIVERPOOL	9/3	26/12	9/12	30/12	24/2	13/4	21/8	—	—	4/5	25/11	4/11	23/3	10/2	13/1	22/10	26/8	22/11	9/9
MAN CITY	17/2	27/4	26/12	30/3	9/3	23/8	10/2	2/12	28/10	—	14/10	9/12	16/9	26/8	18/11	30/12	13/1	23/3	8/4
MAN UTD	4/11	19/8	28/8	24/2	21/10	9/9	24/12	17/12	6/4	4/5	—	25/11	23/9	16/3	13/4	1/1	20/1	3/2
MIDDLESBRO	20/8	23/3	16/12	9/9	3/2	24/2	26/12	30/3	27/4	23/9	28/10	—	30/8	30/12	2/12	15/10	20/1	8/4	9/3	18/11
NEWCASTLE	23/3	18/11	8/4	22/8	9/12	13/1	1/10	27/4	24/2	26/12	10/2	9/3	—	27/8	9/9	29/10	30/12	3/12
NOTTS FOREST	29/8	23/9	18/11	2/12	20/1	8/4	24/2	16/12	1/1	27/4	16/3	23/12	28/10	—	2/3	19/8	14/10	3/2	30/3
QPR	26/12	30/12	19/8	23/3	13/4	22/11	16/9	30/8	3/2	30/12	6/4	4/5	—	—	17/2	4/11	9/12	25/11	20/1
SHEFF WED	21/11	30/12	20/1	21/10	4/11	25/11	30/9	19/8	13/4	6/4	3/2	26/12	9/9	—	9/3	—	24/2	4/5	30/8
SOUTHAMPTON	23/9	8/4	14/10	4/10	1/1	16/9	10/2	26/8	2/1	18/11	12/9	17/2	23/12	—	30/3	23/12	2/3	28/10	16/12
TOTTENHAM	13/4	30/3	30/12	11/11	21/10	25/11	4/11	3/2	17/2	6/4	25/9	16/9	26/12	—	30/8	16/12
WEST HAM	16/9	30/3	2/12	17/2	2/3	9/12	13/1	1/1	8/4	13/1	16/3	27/4	28/10	30/9	10/2	—	16/10
WIMBLEDON	30/12	16/9	13/1	25/11	9/3	23/3	9/12	17/2	4/11	22/11	26/12	13/4	21/10	23/8	26/8	4/11	4/5	30/9	10/2	6/4

ARSENAL FC

Club Number: 0171-226 0304
Tickets: 0171-354 5404
Club Call: 0891-20 20 20
*Calls cost 39p/min. cheap, 49p/min. other times

Arsenal Stadium
Avenell Road
Highbury
London N5 1BU

Arsenal Museum
Fri: 9.30am - 4pm Open to All
Match Days/Eves:
2 hours before kick-off,
North Bank ticket holders only
Cost: £2 Adults, £1 U16s & S.C.
Located at North Bank Stand

Stadium Tours
Mon-Fri: 11am - 1pm
£4 Adults, £2 U-16s & S.C.
Info: Joanne Harney,
Tel: 0171-226 0304

The Gunners Shop
Located by East Stand
Mon-Fri: 9.30am - 5pm
Sat. Match Days: 10.30am - 5.30pm,
closed during the game
Sun. Match Days: 10.30am - kickoff,
plus 45 mins. after game
Match Eves: 9.30am - kickoff,
plus 45 mins. after game
Tel: 0171-226 9562
Fax: 0171-226 0329
<u>Mail Order Service:</u>
Tel: 0171-354 8397

Arsenal World of Sport
Finsbury Park Station
Mon-Sat: 9.30am - 6pm
Tue: 10am - 6pm
Sat. Matches: 9.30am - 6pm
Sun. Matches: 10.30am - 6pm,
closed during the game
Match Eves: 9.30am - 10.30pm,
closed during the game
Next to Finsbury Park Tube
Tel: 0171-272 1000
Fax: 0171-226 0329

TICKETS

Booking Information
General Enquiries: 0171-354 5404
Recorded Information: 0171-359 0131
Credit Card Bookings: 0171-413 3366
Travel Club: 0171-359 0205
Junior Gunners Club: 0171-226 0304

Special Packages
Restaurant Facilities: 0171-704 8165
Corporate Hospitality & Sponsorship Packages:
Match Day Packages: £120 + VAT
Private Lounges: £2,000 + VAT
Sponsorship Packages from £500 + VAT
contact Philip Carling or Yvette Brown:
0171-359 0808

Match Day Prices Season 1995/96

East & West Stand
Upper Tier Centre Blocks	£25 (limited)
Upper Tier Next to Centre	£18 (limited)
Upper Tier Wing Blocks	£16
Lower Tier Wing Blocks	£11.50
Lower Tier Centre Blocks	£12.50

North Bank Stand
Upper Tier Centre Block	£19
Upper Tier Wing Blocks	£15
Lower Tier Centre Block	£15
Lower Tier Wing Blocks	£12

Clock End Stand £11

Family Enclosure (Members Only)
Adults £11.50 (BlockN) £12.50 (BlockO)
Concessions £5 - £5.50

STADIUM

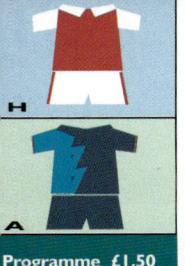

Programme £1.50
Official Magazine
Gunners £2.00
Fanzines
One Nil Down, Two
One Up £1.00
The Gooner £1.00
An Imperfect Match £1.00

NORTH BANK
Level 1
A.F.C Shop
Amusement-
Arcade
Fast Food
Gunners Bar
Ladbrokes
Programme Sales
Ticket Sales
Toilets
Level 2
Arsenal Museum
Bond-Holders'
Restaurant
Level 3
Snack Bars
Toilets
Level 4
Customer Care
Fast Food
Ladbrokes
Licensed Bar
Toilets

EAST STAND
Upper Level
Bagel Junction
Middle & Lower Level
Fast Food
Ladbrokes
Licensed Bar
Toilets
WEST STAND
Upper Level
Bagel Junction
Middle & Lower Level
Fast Food
Ladbrokes
Licensed Bar
Toilets
CLOCK END
Fast Food
Ladbrokes
Licensed Bar
Toilets

VISITORS ENCLOSURE
FAMILY ENCLOSURE
DISABLED ENCLOSURE

HIGHBURY HILL
WEST STAND (Seats 10,500)

| £16 | £18 | £25 | £18 | £16 | UPPER |
| £12.50 | | | | | LOWER |

CLOCK END (Seats 6,500)
Boxes £11

EAST STAND ENCLOSURE
LOWER: £11.50 £12.50 £11.50
UPPER: £16 £18 £25 £18 £16

NORTH BANK (Seats 12,400) GILLESPIE ROAD
£12	£15
£15	£19
£12	£15
LOWER TIER / UPPER TIER

Disabled Access
92 Wheelchairs
1 Helper per person

EAST STAND (Seats 9,500)
AVENELL ROAD

ARSENAL

GETTING TO THE GAME

Arsenal is situated in North London, three miles from the city centre. Plentiful transport access makes it an easy journey from all points. As with many other inner-city grounds, parking during a match is not recommended as parking restrictions come into force. However, one notable exception is the Fonthill Road area (see map): there are limited restrictions and it is worth checking out. For evening matches, Caledonian Road is a good area to park and only two stops away by tube.

BY CAR

From the **North**: Get onto the M1, follow the signs to London and exit at the A1 turn-off - Junction 2 - follow the signs to the City. The A1 merges for a stretch with the A406. Keep to the A1, soon called Archway Road and then Holloway road, for about six miles. After Holloway Road Station, take the third left turn - Drayton Park. ¾ mile on, turn right into Aubert Park and third left into Avenell Road.

From the **North-West**: Follow the M40, turning off at Junction 1, the A40. The A40 becomes Western Avenue and then the Westway. At Angel turn left along Upper Street to Highbury Roundabout. Then same as from the South.

From the **South**: The A3 and the A2 merge into the A3 approaching London Bridge. On the north side of the river the A3 becomes the A10. Follow signs to Bank of England and then to Angel. Go right at the traffic lights (signposted *North*) to Highbury Roundabout, one mile on. Either take St. Paul's Rd exit, turning left into Highbury Grove and then fifth left into Aubert Park, second right into Avenell Rd. Or, take Holloway Rd. exit and third right into Drayton Park, right into Aubert Park, third left into Avenell Road.

From the **West**: From the M4, exit junction 1 to Chiswick, the A315. After 1½ miles turn left into Goldhawk Road (A402). At Shepherds Bush, follow signs around green to *City* to join the M41 for a mile. Turn right onto Westway (A40(M)) and the Ring Road (A501). At Angel turn left to Highbury Roundabout.
Then same as from the South.

From the **East**: From M11/A11 turn right into South End Road (A406) and left into Forest Road (A503) which becomes Ferry Lane. After Tottenham Hale tube station turn left into the Hale and round into Broad Lane, following through onto Seven Sisters Road. At the end of Finsbury Park turn left into Blackstock Road. Take the third right, Ambler Road which becomes Avenell Road.

BY TRAIN

Arsenal Underground Station is at Gillespie Road, adjacent to the stadium.
The nearest Network SouthEast stations are Drayton Park and Finsbury Park.
Kings Cross - Piccadilly Line to Arsenal
Euston - Victoria/Northern Line to Kings Cross, Piccadilly Line to Arsenal
Paddington - Circle/Hammersmith & City Line to Kings Cross, Piccadilly Line to Arsenal
Victoria - Victoria Line to Green Park, Piccadilly Line to Arsenal
Waterloo - Northern Line to Leicester Square, Piccadilly Line to Arsenal

BY BUS

43, 271: Holloway Road
4, 19, 236: Highbury Grove

IN THE AREA

RADIO
London Radio - 97.3 FM & 1152 AM: 24-hour extensive sports coverage seven days a week, twice an hour - previews, results, reviews.

Radio 5 Live - 909 MW General sports coverage - live commentary on main matches plus regular updated bulletins.

TOBY RESTAURANTS
Orange Tree
Totteridge Lane, Totteridge, N20 8NX, tel: 0181-445 6542.
Cafe Gioconda
60 St. John's Wood High Street, St. John's Wood, NW8 7SH, tel: 0171-722 5572.
Jack Straw's Castle
North End Way, Hampstead Heath, NW3 7ES, tel: 0171-435 8885.

HOTELS
Holiday Inn
153 ensuite rooms, bar, restaurant, free parking, Garden Court, Tilling Road, Brent Cross, London NW2 1LP, tel: 0181-455 4777, from £72 per double room, incl. breakfast.

TAXIS
Arsenal Cars
2a Roman Way, N7 8XG, tel: 0171-700 2020.

RESTAURANTS
May Malay
326 Holloway Road, N7, tel: 0171-700 0271
Indian Ocean Tandoori
359 Holloway Rd, N7, tel: 0171-607 0801

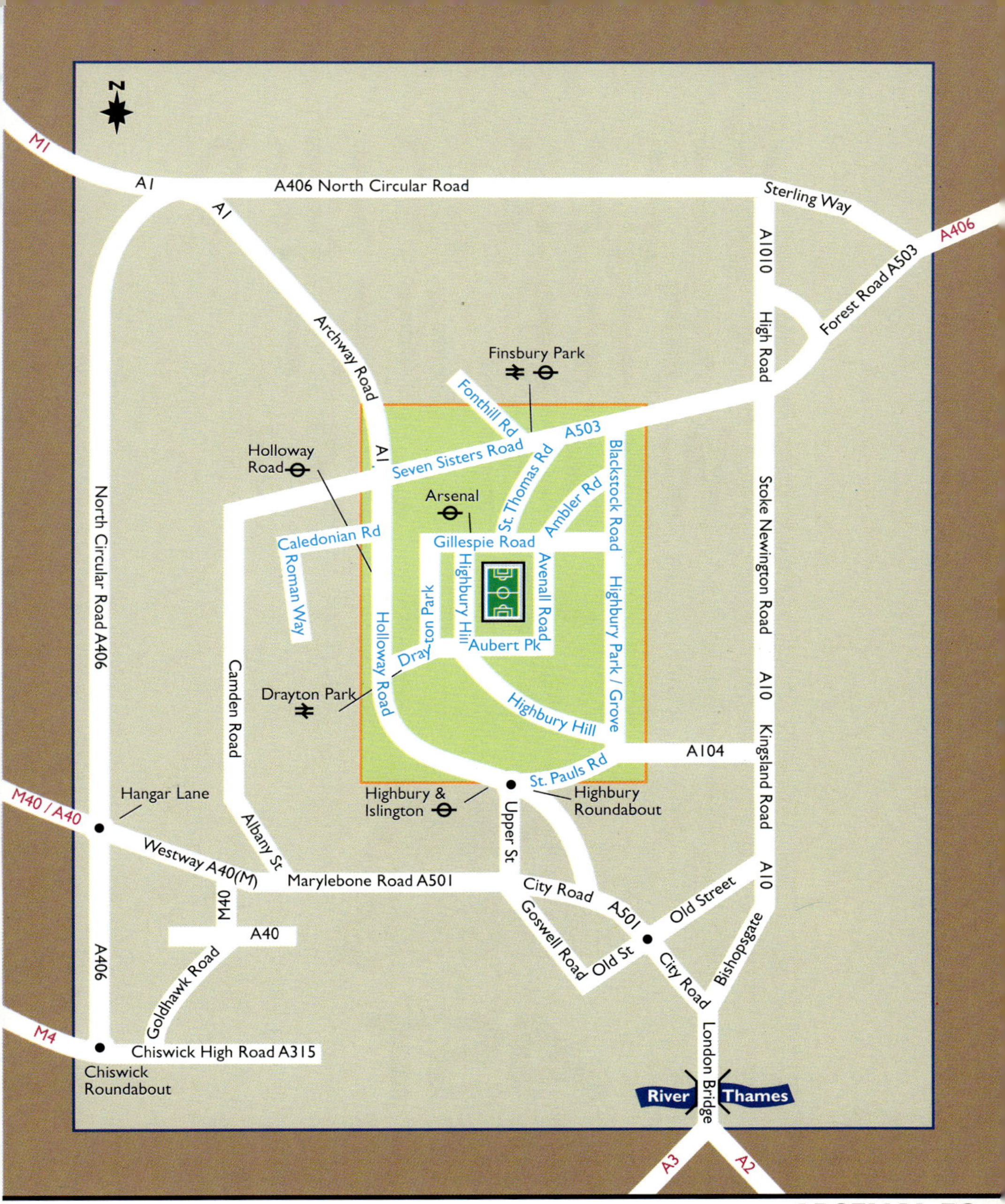
N
M1
A1
A406 North Circular Road
Sterling Way
A406
A1
A1010
Forest Road A503
High Road
Archway Road
Finsbury Park
Fonthill Rd
A503
Seven Sisters Road
A1
Holloway Road
St. Thomas Rd
Blackstock Road
Ambler Rd
Arsenal
Caledonian Rd
Gillespie Road
Roman Way
Highbury Hill
Avenall Road
Drayton Park
Aubert Pk
Highbury Park / Grove
Stoke Newington Road
North Circular Road A406
Camden Road
Holloway Road
Drayton Park
Highbury Hill
A10
A104
Kingsland Road
St. Pauls Rd
Highbury & Islington
Highbury Roundabout
Hangar Lane
M40 / A40
Upper St
Albany St
Westway A40(M)
Marylebone Road A501
City Road
A501
Old Street
A10
M40
A40
Goswell Road
Old St
City Road
Bishopsgate
Goldhawk Road
A406
M4
Chiswick High Road A315
Chiswick Roundabout
London Bridge
River
Thames
A3
A2

ARSENAL FC

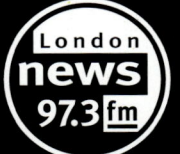

VILLA FIND THE NET WITH AST

Best wishes to Aston Villa for a successful season from their number one sponsor.

For more information on AST products and to find the Net yourself, call 0181 232 5000 or access us at Internet: ASTUK.MAIL@AST.COM

ASTON VILLA FC

Club Number: 0121-327 2299
Tickets: 0121-327 5353
Club Call: 0891-12 11 48
*Calls cost 39p/min. cheap, 49p/min. other times

Villa Park
Trinity Road
Birmingham B6 6HE

Aston Villa Souvenir Shop
Villa Park Stadium
Mon-Fri: 9.30am - 5pm
Sat. Match Days: 9.30am - 3pm,
plus 75 mins after the game
Sun. Match Days: 10am - 4pm,
plus 60 mins after the game
Match Eves: 9.30am - 7.45pm,
plus 30 mins after the game
Tel: 0121-327 2800
Fax: 0121-327 7227
Mail Order Service:
Tel: 0121-327 5963

TICKETS

Booking Information
General Enquiries: 0121-327 5353
Recorded Information: 0891-12 18 48*
Credit Card Bookings: 0121-327 7373
Travel Club: 0121-328 2246

Special Packages
Restaurant Facilities available in the Executive Club, open Mon-Fri to General public, Sat. Match days to sponsors only
Stadium Tours, Mon-Fri: 10.30am - 1.30pm; Match Days: Sponsors only
Corporate Hospitality & Sponsorship Packages, contact Sharon McCullagh: 0121-327 5399

Match Day Prices Season 1995/96

	Adult	Juv/Sen.Cit.
Trinity Road Stand		
Upper Tier	£15	£8
Lower Tier	£13	£7
Doug Ellis Stand		
Upper Tier	£15	£8
Lower Tier	£13	£7
Holte End Stand		
Upper Tier	£13	£6.50
Lower Tier	£12	£5
North Stand		
Upper & Lower Tiers	£13	£6.50

STADIUM

Programme £1.50

Official Magazine
Claret & Blue £2.50

Fanzines
Heroes & Villains £1
The Holy Trinity 50p
The Villa Bugle £1

Disabled Access
Trinity Road Lower: 9 Wheelchairs, 1 Helper per person;
Holte End: 20 Wheelchairs, 1 Helper per person.

TRINITY ROAD STAND
Seats 9,011
Fast Food
Ladbrokes
Licensed Bar
Programmes
Snack Bar (Lower Tier)
Souvenir Kiosk
Toilets
Disabled Toilets (Lower Tier)

DOUG ELLIS STAND
Seats 9,639
Fast Food
Ladbrokes
Licensed Bar
Programmes
Snack Bar
Souvenir Kiosk
Toilets

HOLTE END
Seats 13,577
Fast Food
Ladbrokes
Licensed Bar
Programmes
Snack Bar
Souvenir Kiosk
Toilets

NORTH STAND
Seats 6,876
Fast Food
Ladbrokes
Licensed Bar
Programmes
Snack Bar
Souvenir Kiosk
Toilets

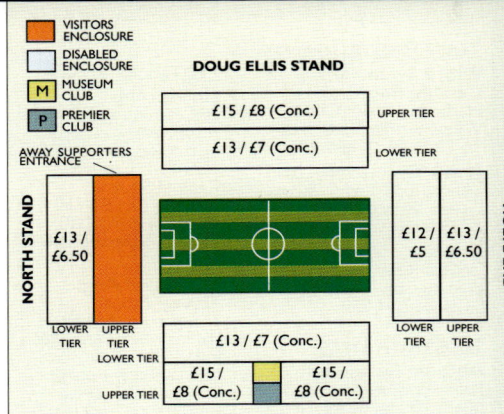

ASTON VILLA

Getting to the Game

Villa Park is situated two miles north of Birmingham City Centre. There are plenty of parking areas in the vicinity of the ground, but visiting supporters should be aware that Away accommodation is in 'R' block which is only accessible from Witton Lane. The visiting supporters coach park is located across the road from 'R' block turnstiles on Witton Lane. The best private parking is on the Witton and Perry Barr side of the ground. A traffic exclusion safety zone is implemented on the two roads either side of the ground, Witton Lane and Trinity Road. This normally commences one hour before kick-off and immediately after the match and a diversion route will be in operation.

By Car

From the **North, South, East & West:** From the M6, exit at Junction 6, following signs to Birmingham NE. At the roundabout, take the fifth exit, signposted Aston, the A5127 Lichfield Road. After a third of a mile, turn right into Aston Hall Road. Pass underneath the expressway until you reach the T-junction with Witton Lane (A4040). Turn right. Villa Park is on your left.

Alternative route from the **West:** From the M5, exit at Junction 1 for the A45 Birmingham Road. Keep to the left fork into Island Road (A4040) and continue for 3 miles, crossing over Walsall Road (A34). At the fourth roundabout, leave the A4040, going straight over into Witton Lane. Villa Park is on the right.

By Train

Regular train services run from Birmingham New Street (0121-643 2711) to Witton Station, where Away supporters are advised to alight. The line also serves Aston Station where the majority of Aston Villa fans travelling by train will alight.

By Bus

Bus information: 0121-200 2700. Catch the No. 7 from town. Specials also operate, tel: 0121-200 7448.

In The Area

Radio

Radio Xtra - 1152 AM: Fri 6pm - 7.30pm Football phone-in; Sat 2pm - 6pm Sports Xtra Live commentary, results, interviews with players & managers, phone-in.

BBC Radio WM - 95.6 FM: 2 - 6pm Sat., 'Sports on Saturday' live match coverage and reviews, plus mid-week live match special, 7 - 10pm.

Toby Restaurants

White Swan Tony Carving Room
Harborne Road, Chad Valley, Birmingham, B15 3TT, tel: 0121-454 2359.

Barnt Green Toby Grill
Kendall End Road, Barnt Green, Birmingham, B45 8PZ, tel: 0121-445 4949.

Towers
Walsall Road, Great Barr, Birmingham, B42 1EY, tel: 0121-357 4112.

Restaurants

Antonio Restaurant
Italian cuisine, from £13 per head, 10 Holloway Circus, Smallbrook, Queensway, B1 1BT, tel: 0121-643 0101.

Bobby Browns
A large vaulted cellar with fireplaces and minstrel's gallery, trendy, noisy, Left Bank, 78/79 Broad Street, B15 1AH, tel: 0121-643 4464.

China Court
Seafood specialities, from £13 per head, 24 Lady-well Walk, B5 4ST, tel: 0121-666 7031.

Pizza Hut
16-18 Cromwell Road, tel: 0121-236 7808.

Hotels / B&B

Holiday Inn
284 ensuite rooms, restaurant, bar, health club, mod. facilities, free overnight parking, Central Square, Birmingham B1 1HH, tel: 0121-631 2000, from £69 per double room.

The Royal Angus Thistle Hotel
133 ensuite rooms, Raffles restaurant, bar, lounge, mod. facilities, free overnight parking, St. Chads, Queensway, B4 6HY, tel: 0121-236 4211, from £35 single, £79 double per night.

Forte Posthouse
192 rooms, restaurant, bar, all mod. cons., fitness centre, pool, sauna, Chapel Lane, Great Barr, B43 2BG, tel: 0121-357 7444, from £42 per person per night.

Hagley Court Hotel
27 rooms, restaurant, bar, all mod. cons., 229 Hagley Road, Edgbaston, B16 9RP, tel: 0121-454 6514, from £30 per person per night.

Places to Visit

Stirchley Superbowl
10-pin bowling centre, 32 lanes, also Quasar space, licensed bars, fast food diner, conferences catered for, Pershore Road, Stirchley, B30 2BY, tel: 0121-458 4444, Open Mon-Fri: 12 - 7pm, Sat-Sun: 10am - 2pm, Adults £2.35, Juniors £1.85.

Cadbury World
The wide world of chocolate, history, development, and yes plenty of samples, Linden Road, Bournville, B30 2LD, tel: 0121-451 4180, Open 7 days, 10am - 5.30pm, Adults £4.90, Juniors £3.35, Under 5's free.

Dry Ski Slope
Ackers Trust, Golden Hillock Road, Small Heath, B11 2PY, tel: 0121-771 4448, Adults £9.50, Juniors £6.50, includes instructor and equipment for one hour; for the experienced skier, Adults £6, Juniors £4.

Warwick Castle
Built in 1068 by William the Conqueror, an outstanding medieval castle, 45 minutes by car, Warwick, CV34 4QU, tel: 01926 408 000, Open 7 days, 10am - 4.30pm, Adults £8.25, Juniors £4.95.

Tourist Information Centre: 0121-643 2514

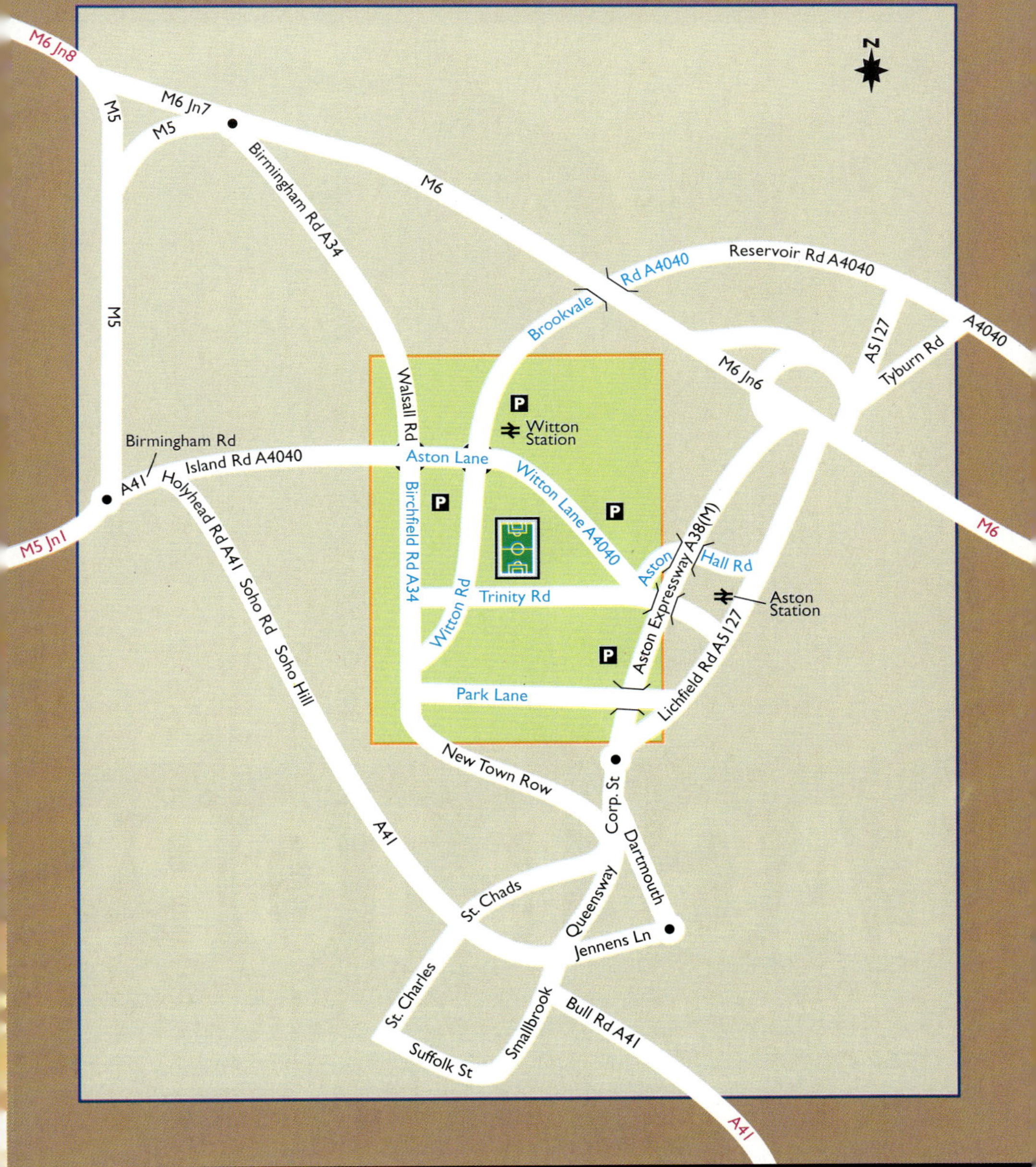

ASTON VILLA FC

1st
- WITH THE VILLA NEWS
- WITH THE RESULTS
- WITH INTERVIEWS

XTRA 1152 SPORT am

FOR THE VERY BEST COVERAGE OF ASTON VILLA FC IT HAS TO BE SPORTS XTRA WITH TOM ROSS AND IAN CROCKER 1152 AM ON THE MEDIUM WAVE

LAGER TOPS

The Scottish and English Premier Championships have witnessed a unique double. Rangers – Champions in Scotland. Blackburn Rovers – Champions in England. And for the first time in history, the winners of both titles carry the same name on their shirts – McEwan's Lager.

THE SCOTTISH AND ENGLISH CHAMPIONS AND THEIR PROUD SPONSOR McEWAN'S LAGER – AN ALIVE AND KICKING COMBINATION.

ALIVE *AND* KICKING

BLACKBURN ROVERS FC

Club Number: 01254-698 888
Tickets: 01254-696 767
Club Call: 0891-12 11 79
*Calls cost 39p/min. cheap, 49p/min. other times

**Ewood Park
Blackburn
Lancashire
BB2 4JF**

Roverstore
Ewood Park Stadium
Mon-Fri: 9am - 5.30pm
Sat: 9am - 4pm, Sun: 11am - 4pm
Match Eves: 9am - kickoff,
plus 20 mins after the game
Tel: 01254-665 606
Fax: 01254-673 523
Mail Order Service:
Tel: 01254-672 137

TICKETS

Booking Information

General Enquiries: 01254-696 767
Recorded Information: 0891-12 10 14*
Credit Card Bookings: 01254-696 767
Travel Club: 01254-698 888, ex.2208

Special Packages

Conferences and Banqueting,
contact Janet O'Halloran: 01254-697 900
New Stadium Tours
contact Jill Haisley: 01254-699 8888, ext 2218
Corporate Hospitality & Sponsorship Packages,
contact Ken Beamish
or Linda Sweet: 01254-661 177

Match Day Prices Season 1995/96

	Adult	Jun./Sen.
Jack Walker Stand		
Upper Tier Central	£17.50	
Upper Tier Outer	£16.50	£8
Lower Tier Central	£16.50	£8
Lower Tier Outer	£14	£7
Walker Steel Stand	£14	£7
Darwen End		
Lower Tier	£14	£7
Upper Tier	£14	£7
Blackburn End		
Lower Tier	£14	£7
Upper Tier Family Stand	£14	£7
(Under 8 Free; Min. purchase 1 Adult + 1 Junior)		

STADIUM

Programme £1.50
Official Magazine
Rovers Magazine
Monthly
£2

Disabled Access
140 Wheelchairs,
1 Helper per person.

JACK WALKER STAND
Seats 11,000
Executive Lounges
Fast Food
Ladbrokes
Licensed Bar
Snack Bar
Toilets
No Smoking in the Stand

WALKER STEEL STAND
Seats 5,000
Fast Food
First Aid Station
Ladbrokes
Snack Bar
Toilets

DARWEN END
Seats 8,000
Fast Food
International Suite
Ladbrokes
Snack Bars
Toilets

BLACKBURN END
Seats 8,000
Fast Food
Ladbrokes
Snack Bar
Toilets
Macdonalds
Strikers Restaurant
(Upper Tier; No Smoking)

BLACKBURN ROVERS

GETTING TO THE GAME

Blackburn Rovers are situated a mile from Blackburn town centre in Ewood Park. Car Parking can be found at Albion Road and Hollin Bridge Street, the earlier, the better chance of finding a space. Otherwise, park in town and bus in. Buses run frequently from the Bus Station to the Ground.

BY CAR

From the **North and West**: Leave the M6 at Junction 31, taking the A677 to Blackburn. After approx. 3½ miles, at the junction with traffic lights and Esso garage, turn right into Montague Street. At King Street, turn right and then first left into Byrom Street. Take the third right into Canterbury Street and right again into Freckleton Street. At the end turn right into Bolton Road. Ewood Park is a mile along, on the left.

For free parking: after turning into Great Bolton Street, continue for half a mile and turn right into Hollin Bridge Street.

Alternative route from the **North and West**: Leave the M6 at Junction 31 onto the A677 and follow into town. After approx. 5 miles turn left along Barbara Castle Way, right into Penny Street, right into Church Street and left into Darwen Street, which becomes Bolton Road.

From the **South**: Either as above for North and West, Or: Take the A666 to Blackburn from Bolton. This becomes Bolton Road at Darwen. After 1½ miles, Ewood Park is on your right. Follow the one way system left into Livesey Branch Road and take the first right Albion Road where there is a car park.

From the **East**: Using the A679, follow straight and turn left at Great Bolton Street (A666). This becomes Bolton Street; after 1¼ miles Ewood Park is to your left. Turn right into Livesey Branch Road and first right into Albion Road for the car park.
Using the A677: At junction with A679 (Accrington Road) turn left, then as above.

BY TRAIN

Blackburn Railway Station (01254 662537) is situated adjacent to the town centre, approx 1½ miles from the ground. Alternatively, alight at Mill Hill Station: a ten-minute walk to the ground.

BY BUS

The Central Bus Station is directly opposite the Railway Station and buses to the ground run from Bus Shelter P, nos. 3, 4, 346, every 10 minutes.

IN THE AREA

RADIO

Red Rose Radio - 999 AM: Sat 2pm - 6pm 'Saturday Sport' live comentary, reports from local matches, interviews with players and managers; Sat & Sun 7.30pm & 8.30pm bulletins.

BBC Radio Lancashire - 95.5 FM, 103.9AM - Fri 6 - 10pm, sports coverage including 2 hours of soccer news/views. Sat.: 2 - 6pm coverage of local matches and league round-ups.

TOBY RESTAURANTS

Waterfront Toby Restaurant
Navigation Way, Rivers Way, Preston Dock, Preston, PR2 2YP, tel: 01772-721 108.

White Bear
Ginburn Road, Barrowford, Nelson, Lancs. BB9 6EG, tel: 01282-615 646.

Ye Olde Sparrow Hawk
Wheatley Lane, Fence, Burnley, Lancs BB12 9QG, tel: 01282-614 126.

RESTAURANTS

Blakeys Cafe Bar
Under £13 per head, King George's Hall, Northgate, BB1 2AA, tel: 01254-667021

The Moorings
From £10 per head, on the Canal, Bolton Road, BB2 3PZ, opposite the Infirmary, tel: 01254-664 472

Red House Motel & Restaurant
Around £15 per head, Cravens Brow, Bolton Road, BB2 4LA, tel: 01254-53838

HOTELS / B&B

The Stirk House Hotel
45 en-suite rooms, mod. facilities, restaurant Gisburn, nr. Clitheroe, BB7 4LJ, tel: 01200-445 581
Single £35, Double £58 (incl. breakfast)

Red House Ravenscroft
20 rooms, mod. cons., restaurant, Cravens Brow, BB2 4LA, tel: 01254-53838
Single £24, Double £38 (incl. breakfast)

Aucklands
Preston New Road, BB2 6BH, tel: 01254-53309
Double or Single £14 per person per night, (incl. dinner & breakfast)

PLACES TO VISIT

Waves Water Fun Centre
Nab Lane, BB2 1LN, tel: 01254-51111
Luxury leisure swimming pool with giant flume, wave machine, 20 person spa, sunbeds, cafeteria, Adults £2.40, Juniors, £1.90 juniors, free parking.

The Chocolate House
1, Glenfield Park, Philips Road, BB1 5PF, tel: 01254-581 019
Hand-made chocolates workroom and shop.

Witton Country Park & Visitor Centre
480 acres of beautiful countryside, good facilities Preston Old Road, BB2 2TP, tel: 01254-55423, open 7 days.

Tommy Ball's Shoe Shop
The biggest shoe warehouse in Britain Hart Street, BIB1 1HW, tel: 01254-261 910, open 7 days.

The Blackburn Waterside
Picturesque canal running through town. Info: 01254-56557

Blackburn Arena Ice Skating Rink
Park Road, BB1 1BB, tel: 01254-263 063
Open 7 days, 10am - 11pm, admission £2.75 - £4.50

County Information Centre: 01254-681 120

Tourist Information Centre: 01254-53277

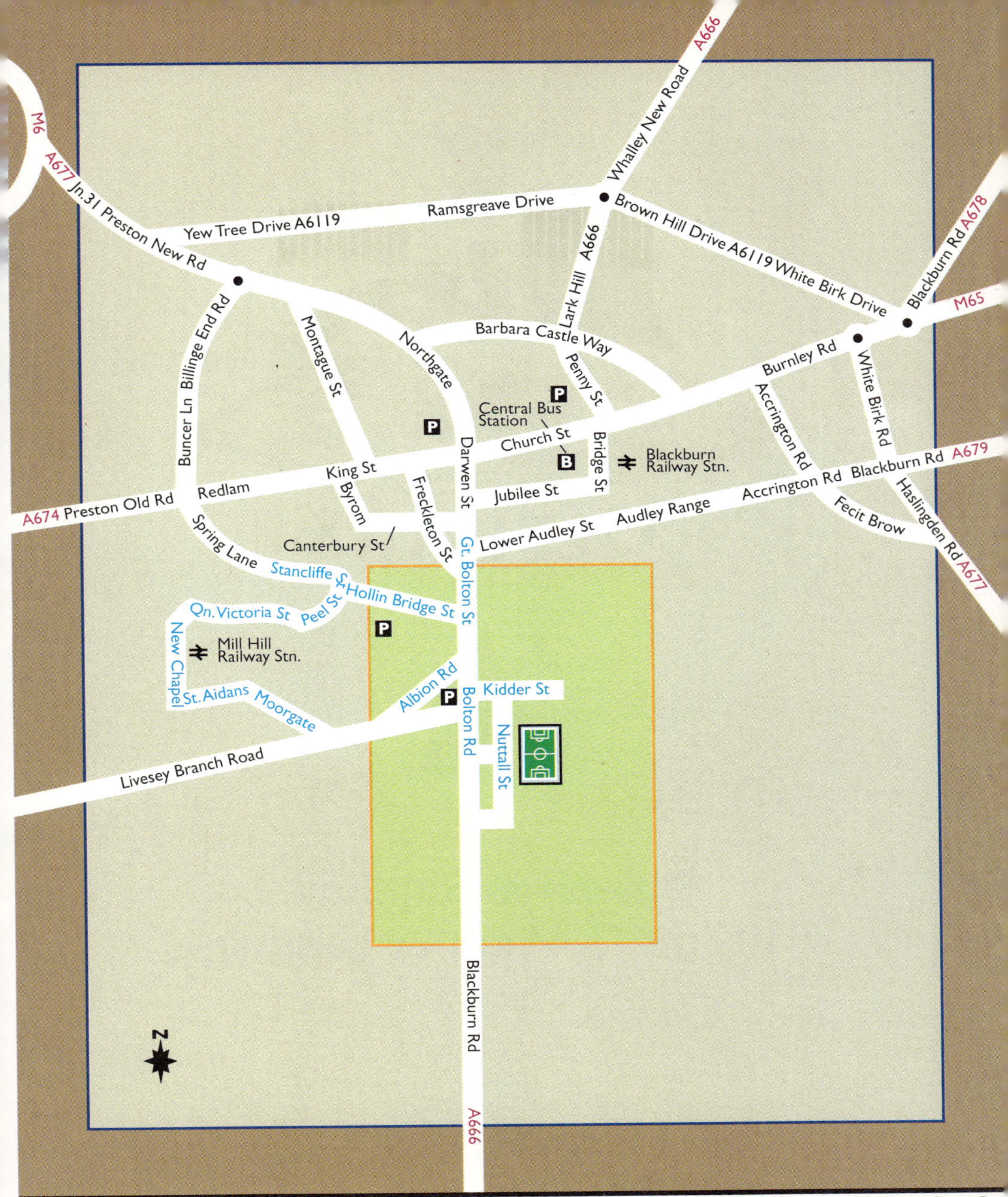

BLACKBURN ROVERS FC

THE LIVE ACTION STATION

**Official match ball
of the FA Premier League
from**

The market leader in footballs

BOLTON WANDERERS FC

Club Number: 01204-389 200
Tickets: 01204-521 101
Club Call: 0891-12 11 64
*Calls cost 39p/min. cheap, 49p/min. other times

Burnden Park
Manchester Road
Bolton
Lancashire BL3 2QR

Burnden Sports
Burnden Park Stadium
Mon-Fri: 10am - 5pm
Sat/Sun Match Days & Match Eves:
10am - kickoff & 30 mins. after game
Tel: 01204-389 200, Fax: 01204 382 334

The Centre Spot
Crompton Place, Bradshawgate, Bolton
Tel: 01204-391 062
Mon-Fri: 9.30am - 5.30pm

TICKETS

Booking Information

General Enquiries: 01204-389 200
Credit Card Bookings: 01204-521 101
Travel Club: 01204-524 518
Junior Whites, contact Bill Longden: 01204-381 010
Football in the Community: 01204-364 555
Burnden Sporting Initiative: 01204-381 010

Special Packages

Restaurant Facilities available in the Executive Club
Stadium Tours, contact Geoff Lomax: 01204-364 555
Corporate Hospitality & Sponsorship Packages, contact Graham Eddleston: 01204-389 200

Match Day Prices Season 1995/96

	Adult	Juv/Sen.Cit.
Manchester Road Stand	£15	£9
Manchester Road Terrace	£11	£8
Burnden Stand	£15	£9
Burnden Terrace	£11	£8
Great Lever Stand	£11	£8
Embankment Terrace (Visitors)	£11	

Family Tickets for seats in the Great Lever Stand,
1 Adult + 2 Juveniles: £19.50
2 Adults + 2 Juveniles: £26

STADIUM

Programme £1.50

MANCHESTER ROAD STAND
Seats 2,928
Disabled Area
Snack Bars
Toilets

MANCHESTER ROAD TERRACE
Seats 2,540
First Aid Station
Snack Bar
Toilets

BURNDEN STAND
Seats 2,028
Snack Bars
Toilets

BURNDEN TERRACE
Seats 7,892
Snack Bars
Toilets

GREAT LEVER STAND
Seats 2,935
Snack Bars
Toilets

EMBANKMENT TERRACE
Seats 2,935
Snack Bars
Superstore
Toilets

Disabled Access
Main Door, Manchester Road Stand, 14 Wheelchairs, 1 Helper per person

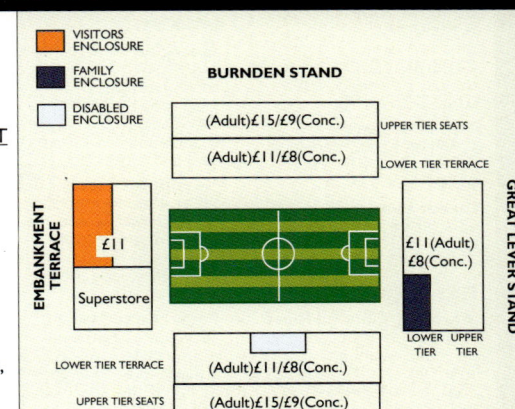

BOLTON WANDERERS

GETTING TO THE GAME

Bolton Wanderers play at Burnden Park Stadium, half a mile from Bolton town centre. It is usually possible to park in the car park by the ground. There is in force a local bye-law, covering the area between the town centre and the ground, which prohibits persons drinking alcohol in the street from any form of container. The public houses in the vicinity of the ground subscribe to a Licensees' alliance and on match days only allow Home Supporters onto the premises.

BY CAR

From the **North:** From the M61, exit at Junction 5 for the Wigan Road (A58). Stay on the A58 as it becomes the A676, and then Deane Road. At the end of Deane Road, turn right into Trinity Street. Pass Bolton Station on your right, and take the right turn into Manchester Road. Burnden Park is ½ mile down the road, on the left.

From the **South, East & West:** From the M62, exit at Junction 14 onto the M61. Follow the M61 into the the M61 spur, and into the Farnworth and Kearsley Bypass (A666). Continue along for 2½ miles to the next slip road after passing the ground on the left. Turn left into Lower Bridgman Street to the automatic traffic signals. Turn left into Manchester Road, and follow for ½ mile to the M.F.I.. Turn left into Scholey Street. The visitors car park is on the right, at the end of Scholey Street. (The car park is monitored by CCTV carmeras)

BY TRAIN

Bolton Railway Station (0161-832 8353) is situated a short walk from Burnden Park.

IN THE AREA

RADIO

Piccadilly Gold Sport - 103 FM, 1152 AM: Sat 1 - 6pm, pre-match and after-match phone-in, plus live commentaries of top local games. Also Sunday pm if Premier League match on.

GMR - 95.1 FM: 2 - 6pm Sat., reporting live from local big games; also 2.30 - 6pm Sun., 7 - 10pm Tue, Wed., if match on, and hourly sports report.

TOBY RESTAURANTS

Squirrel Toby Restaurant
Bispham Road, Greenlands, Blackpool, Lancs. FY2 0LB, tel: 01253-352 198.

The Nab Gate
1 Arthur Lane, Harwood, Bolton, BL2 4JB. tel: 01204-524 034.

Coach House
13 Church Street, Preston, Lancs. PR1 3BQ, tel: 01772-880 850.

RESTAURANTS

Smithalls Coach House
From £4.35 light lunch, £11 per head evenings, Smithalls Dean Road, BL1 7NR, tel: 01204-840 377.

The Spread Eagle
From £6 per head, 10 Bolton Road, Edgworth, near Bolton, BL7 0DF, tel: 01204-852 369.

The Watergate Toll
From £7 per head, 421 Watergate Drive, BL5 1BU, tel: 01204-64989.

HOTELS / B&B

Holiday Inn
303 ensuite rooms, restaurants, bars, indoor pool, Crowne Plaza, Peter Street, Manchester M60 2DS, tel: 0161-228 2241, from £96 per double room, incl. breakfast.

Georgian House Hotel
100 ensuite rooms, all mod. facilities, Manchester Road, Blackrod, BL6 5RU, tel: 01942-814 598, from £60 incl. breakfast.

Beaumont Hotel
96 ensuite rooms, all mod. cons., Beaumont Road, BL3 4TA, tel: 01204-651 511, £40-£60, weekends incl. breakfast.

Pack Horse Hotel
72 ensuite rooms, all mod. cons., Nelson Square, Bradshawgate, BL1 1DP, tel: 01204-527 261, £30-£40 incl. breakfast.

Commercial Royal Hotel
11 rooms, 7 ensuite, mod. cons., 13-15 Bolton Road, Moses Gate, Farnworth, BL4 7JN, tel: 01204-73661, from £25.

PLACES TO VISIT

The Water Place
Aquaflume, Raging River Ride, Health Spa, Wild Water Channel, adventures with the wet stuff, located in the town centre, Great Moor Street, BL1 1SP, tel: 01204-364 616, Open 7 Days, Mon-Fri 10am - 10pm, Thur 10am - 8.30pm, Sat/Sun 10am - 5.30pm, Adults £2.75, Juniors £2.10.

Laser Quest
Ultimate adventure, for all ages, Bradshawgate, BL1 1QD, tel: 01204-388 308, Open 7 Days, Mon-Fri 11am - 10pm, Sat 12pm - 10pm, Sun 11am - 7pm, £3 weekdays, £3.50 weekends & eves.

Hollywood Adventure Playworld
Excellent play facilities for children of all abilities, Great Lever, BL3 6SR, tel: 01204-523 408, Mon-Fri, Under 5's 1-4pm, 5-10's 4-6pm, 50p - £1.

Moss Bank Park & Animal World
72 acres of Moss Bank originally used for the Ainsworth bleaching business. Miniature railway, amphitheatre, children's play area, football pitches and other sports facilities, Moss Bank Way, BL1 5TD, tel: 01204-846 157, Open 7 Days 10am - 4.30pm, free admission.

Warburton's Bread Bakery
Group tours of established, thriving bakery, Hereford Street, BL1 8JB, tel: 01204-523 551, Open Tue, Thur 2.30pm, Mon, Wed, Thur 7.30pm, free admission.

Tourist Information Centre: 01204-364 333

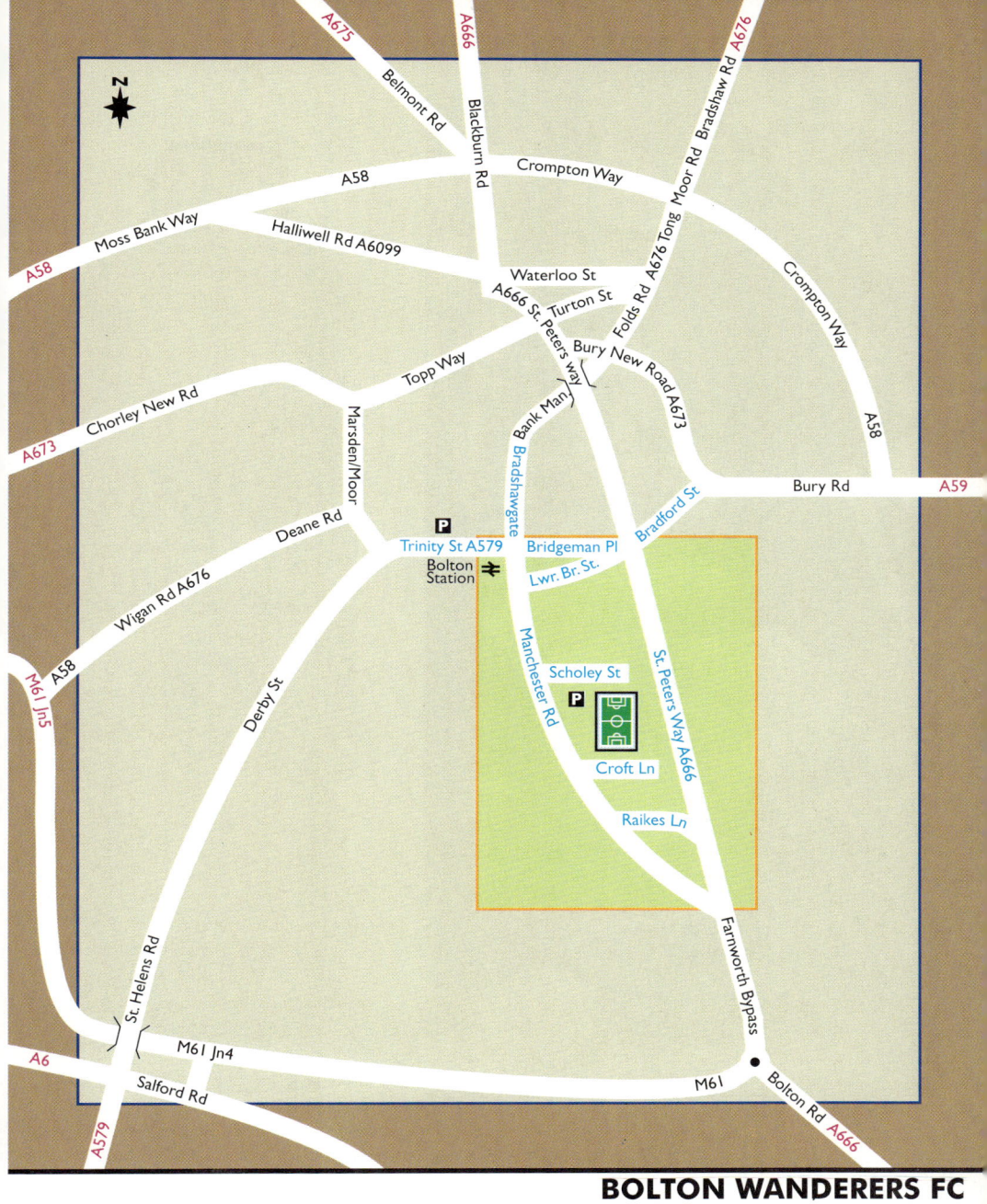

BOLTON WANDERERS FC

For full match commentary — **PICCADILLY RADIO 1152 AM** — **Always number one for sport**

LEGENDS

Peter Osgood is a Chelsea Legend. Few true fans will forget his battles with Leeds United, his crucial diving header in the 1970 FA Cup Final Replay at Old Trafford or that amazing left-footer at Stamford Bridge which the AC Milan goalkeeper probably never saw. It's the same with Coors Extra Gold, the Rocky Mountain Legend. Coors is a full bodied, premium lager with a taste that few true lager fans forget, in cans, bottles and on draught.

Coors is the official sponsor of Chelsea Football Club.

CHELSEA FC

Club Number: 0171-385 5545
Tickets: 0891-12 10 11
Club Call: 0891-12 11 59
*Calls cost 39p/min. cheap, 49p/min. other times

Stamford Bridge
Fulham Road
London
SW6 1HS

Chelsea Sportsland
394-400 Fulham Road
London SW6 1HW
Mon-Fri: 9am - 5pm
Sat. Match Days: 9am - 6pm
Sun. Match Days: 11am - 6.30pm
Match Eves: 9am - 10.30pm
Tel: 0171-381 4569,
Fax: 0171-381 5697
Mail Order Service:
Tel: 0171-381-4569

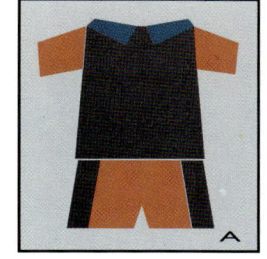

TICKETS

Booking Information
General Enquiries: 0171-385 5545
Credit Card Bookings: 0171-386 7799
Travel Club: 0171-381 5500
Chelsea Pitchowners: 0171-610 2235
Bridge Builder Promotions: 0171-386 5557

Special Packages
Bentley's Restaurant Matchday Packages,
contact the Marketing Department:
0171-385 7809
Stadium Tours, Fridays 11am - 12.30pm:
0171-385 0710
Corporate Hospitality & Sponsorship Packages,
contact Carole Phair, Commercial Manager:
0171-385 7809
Conference & Banqueting,
contact Debra Ware: 0171-385 7980

Match Day Prices Season 1995/96

	Cat. A	Cat. B
North Stand		
Upper Tier (Members Only)	£20	£15
Lower Tier	£20	£15
(Members Only until one week before match)		
West Stand	£20	£13
Western Enclosure	£12 (£6)	£10 (£5)
(Members Only)		
East Stand		
Upper Tier	£25	£16
Middle Tier	£35	£22
Lower Tier	£20	£17
East Stand Family Section		
One Juv/One Adult	£18	£14
Add. Juv/Unaccompanied Juv	£6	£4
Add. Qualifying Adult	£18	£14

Prices in brackets denote concessions for Juniors and Sen. Citizens

STADIUM

Programme £2

Monthly Club Newspaper
Onside 90p

Fanzines
The Chelsea Independent £1
Cockney Rebel 30p
The Red Card 80p

NORTH STAND
Seats 8,600
Drakes Bar & Restaurant (Chelsea Pitch Owners & Season Ticket Holders only)
Dixons & Tamblings Bar (Members only)
Ladbrokes
Snack Bars
Toilets

EAST STAND
Seats 11,160
Bentley's Restaurant
Ossies Tavern (Exec. Members, Box-holders only)
Ladbrokes

EAST STAND FAMILY ENCL.
Seats 2,028
Creches
Food Kiosk
Toilets

WEST STAND
Seats 6,056
Food Kiosk
Ladbrokes
2 Licensed Bars
First Aid Station
Toilets

Disabled Access
East Stand family section, 40 Wheelchairs, 40 Helpers;
North Stand Upper Tier, 5 Wheelchairs, 5 Helpers

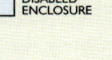
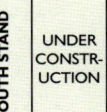

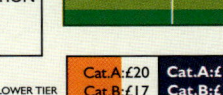

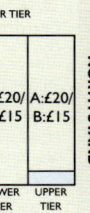

- VISITORS ENCLOSURE
- FAMILY ENCLOSURE
- DISABLED ENCLOSURE

WEST STAND
Cat.A:£20/Cat.B:£13 — UPPER TIER
Members Enclosure Cat.A:£12(£6)/Cat.B:£10(£5) — LOWER TIER

SOUTH STAND — UNDER CONSTRUCTION

NORTH STAND
A:£20/B:£15 LOWER TIER
A:£20/B:£15 UPPER TIER

EAST STAND
LOWER TIER: Cat.A:£20 / Cat.B:£17 — Cat.A:£18 / Cat.B:£14
MIDDLE TIER: Cat.A:£35/Cat.B:£22
UPPER TIER: Cat.A:£325/Cat.B:£16

CHELSEA

GETTING TO THE GAME

Chelsea play at Stamford Bridge, close to the heart of London. Parking is subject to rigorously enforced restrictions, and it is recommended to park across town and come to the ground on the Tube.

BY CAR

From the **North:** Take the M1 to the North Circular Road (A406) westbound and follow for approx. 4 miles to Hangar Lane roundabout. Take the left exit into Western Avenue (A40). Follow for 3½ miles. Do not enter onto the flyover but keep to the left hand lane for the roundabout, and turn right onto the M41. Go over the next roundabout into Holland Rd (A3220) and enter the one way system into Addison Crescent (which becomes Addison Road, Warwick Gardens and Pembroke Road) following the signs to Chelsea. Turn right into Earls Court Road (A3220) and continue straight, crossing over Cromwell Road and Old Brompton Road, into Redcliffe Gardens. At the traffic lights, turn right into Fulham Road. Stamford Bridge is ¼ mile along on the right.

Alternative route: From the M40, continue into the A40, and at Hangar Lane roundabout turn right onto the North Circular Road (A406). Then as above.

From the **South:** Approach via the A3 and turn left into Putney Hill (A219). Cross the Thames on Putney Bridge. Bear left past New Kings Road and then turn right into Fulham Road (A304). Follow this road round for 1 mile, to Stamford Bridge.

Alternative route: From the M23, continue into the A23. Bear left into Tooting Bec Road (A214), and cross over the A3. Continue along Trinity Road, straight over the roundabout and across Wandsworth Bridge (now the A217). In less than a mile you come to a T-junction with the Kings Road. Turn right and then fourth left into Maxwell Rd. Turn right into Fulham Road, Stamford Bridge is on the left.

From the **East:** From the M11, join the North Circular Road (A406) westbound. Continue along for approx. 15 miles until Hangar Lane roundabout. Then same as from the North.

From the **West:** From the M4, continue into the A4. Continue for 3½ miles along the Great West Road, over the Hammersmith flyover, into Talgarth Road, which becomes West Cromwell Road (and further on Cromwell Road). Turn right into Earls Court Road (A3220) and continue straight, crossing over Cromwell Road and Old Brompton Road, into Redcliffe Gardens. At the traffic lights, turn right into Fulham Road. Stamford Bridge is ¼ mile along on the right.

BY TRAIN

The nearest Underground Station is Fulham Broadway on the District Line.
Kings Cross - Victoria Line to Victoria, District Line to Fulham Broadway
Euston - Victoria Line to Victoria, District Line to Fulham Broadway
Paddington - District Line to Fulham Broadway
Victoria - District Line to Fulham Broadway
Waterloo - Northern Line to Embankment, District Line to Fulham Broadway

IN THE AREA

RADIO
London Radio - 97.3 FM & 1152 AM: 24-hour extensive sports coverage seven days a week, twice an hour - previews, results, reviews.
Radio 5 Live - 909 MW General sports coverage - live commentary on main matches plus regular updated bulletins.

TOBY RESTAURANTS
Alleyns Head
Park Hall Road, West Dulwich, London SE21 8BW, tel: 0181-670 6540.

George Whitaker & Son
326 Earls Court Road, London SW5 9BQ, tel: 0171-373 9172.

Feathers
20 Broadway, Westminster, London SW1H 0BH, tel: 0171-222 3744.

RESTAURANTS
Big Easy
From £15 per head, 332 Kings Road, SW3 5UR, tel: 0171-352 4071

Nachos Mexican Restaurant & Cantina
From £15 per head, 212 Fulham Road, SW10 9PJ, tel: 0171-351 7531

Macmillans Brasserie
From £20 per head, 351 Fulham Road, SW10 9TW, tel: 0171-351 2939

HOTELS / B&B
Holiday Inn
162 ensuite rooms, restaurants, bars, leisure facilities, private garden, 100 Cromwell Road, London SW7 4ER, tel: 0171-373 2222, from £165 per double room.

Kenwood House Hotel
16 rooms, 114 Gloucester Place, W1H 3DB, tel: 0171-935 3473, B&B from £27 per person per night.

TAXIS
Atlas Cars
798 Fulham Road, SW6, tel: 0171-602 1234.

K.A.B. Radio Cars
392 Lillie Road, SW6, tel: 0171-352 9999

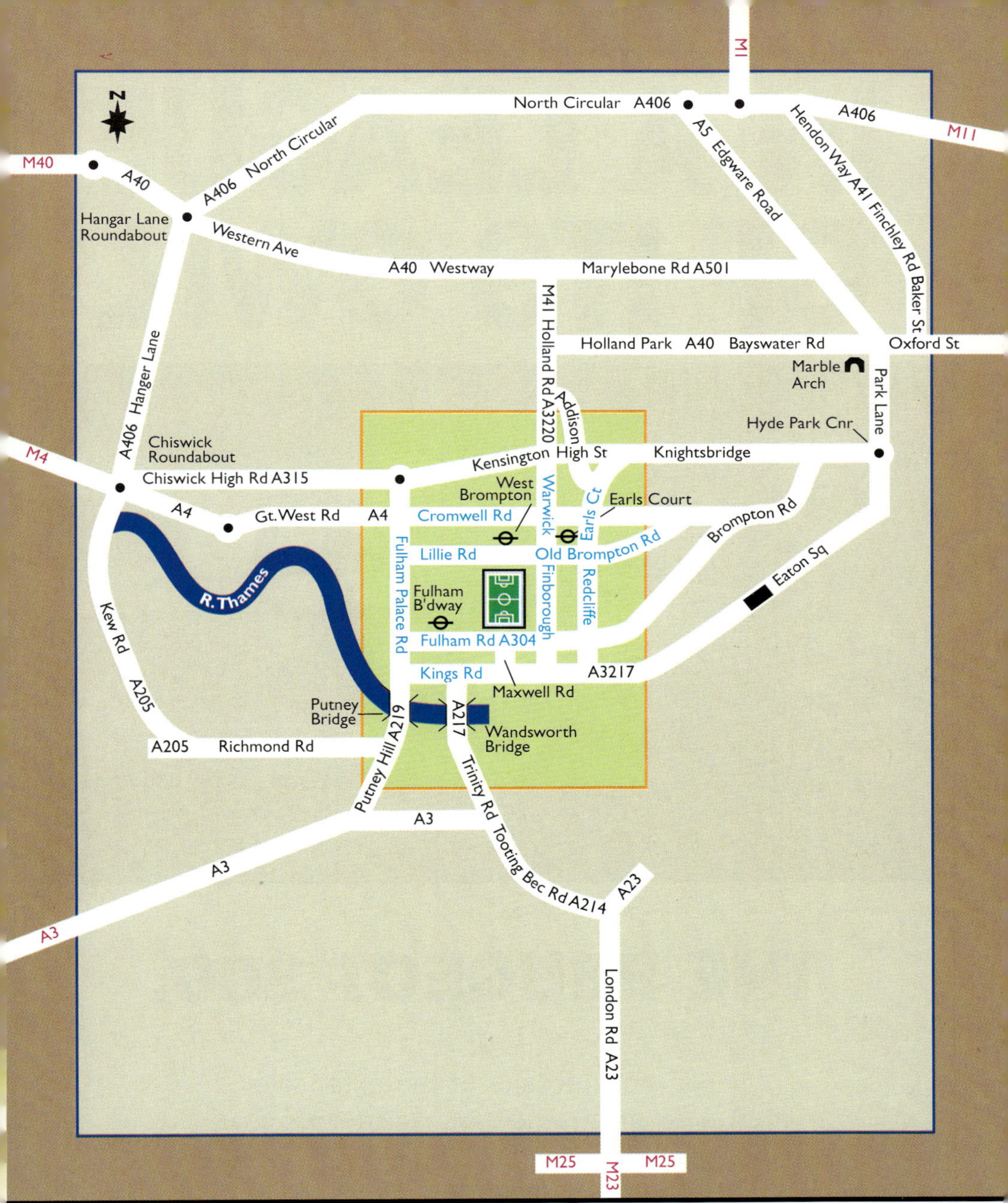

CHELSEA FC

The only sports channel you'll ever need

IN A LEAGUE OF ITS OWN.

THE PEUGEOT 306.

For more details of the extensive
Peugeot 306 range call 0345 22 23 24.

PEUGEOT

COVENTRY CITY FC

Club Number: 01203-223 535
Tickets: 01203-225 545
Club Call: 0891-12 11 66
*Calls cost 39p/min. cheap, 49p/min. other times

**Highfield Road Stadium
King Richard Street
Coventry
CV2 4FW**

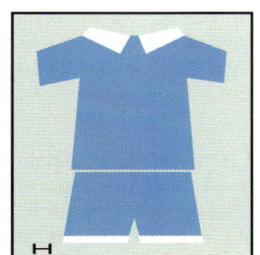

Coventry City FC Shop
Thackhall St, Coventry
Mon-Fri: 9am - 5pm
Sat./Sun. Match Days: 9am - kickoff,
plus 30 mins. after the match
Match Eves: 10am - 10.30pm
Tel: 01203-257 707
Fax: 01203-633 854

Coventry City FC Shop
Cathedral Lane, Coventry
Mon-Fri & Match Sats: 9am - 5.30pm
Tel: 01203-633 619

TICKETS

Booking Information

General Enquiries: 01203-225 545
Recorded Information: 0891-12 11 66*
Credit Card Bookings: 01203-225 545
Ticket Office Fax: 01203-258 856
Travel Club: 01203-225 545

Special Packages

Restaurant Facilities: 01203-631 023
Corporate Hospitality & Matchday Packages, Kit or Steward Sponsorship, The Executive Club, Premier Club & The Vice Presidents Club, plus Matchday Entertainment from £70 per person, contact the Marketing Department: 01203 633 823

Match Day Prices Season 1995/96

	Adult		Jun./Sen.	
	A Grade	B Grade	A Grade	B Grade
Main Stand	£20	£17	£10*	£8.50*
M&B Stand	£18	£15	£9	£7.50
East Stand	£18	£15	£9	£7.50
Co-op Bank Family Stand	£15	£12	£7.50	£6
West Terrace	£15	£12	£7.50	£6
J.S.B. Areas	J.S.B.'s All Matches - £4			
Visitors	£18	£15	£10	£8

*J.S.B. & Senior Citizens, Members only

STADIUM

Programme £1.50

Official Monthly Newspaper
Sky Blue News 26p

MAIN STAND
Seats 3,300
Betting Facilities
Concourse with Snack Bar
Toilets

M&B STAND
Seats 6,800
Food Court
Toilets

EAST STAND
Seats 5,100
Food Court
Toilets

CO-OP BANK FAMILY STAND
Seats 3,200
Kids Area
Ice-cream Bar
Lounge

Snack Counter
Television

WEST TERRACE
Seats 2,800
Betting Facilities
Snack Bar
Toilets

Disabled Access
Thackhall Street Entrance, Clock Stand & M&B Home,
24 Wheelchairs,
47 Helpers

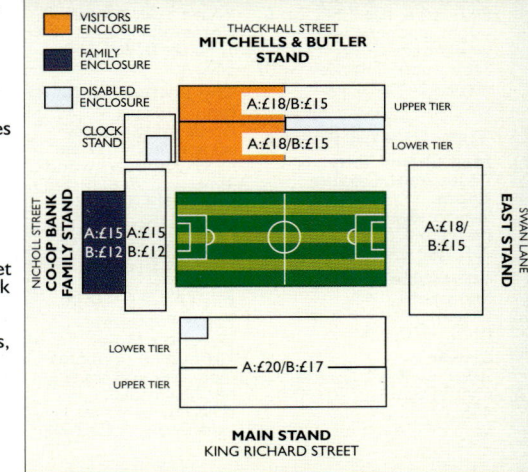

COVENTRY CITY

GETTING TO THE GAME

Coventry City play at the Highfield Road Stadium, less than a mile from the city centre. It is usually possible to find parking off Kingsway, or alternatively there is a car park on your right as you come off the Ringway into Sky Blue Way. Please note, Swan Lane is closed to traffic one hour before the match.

BY CAR

From the **North:** Take the M1 to Junction 21, and join the M69, and then the M6. Just before the end of the M6, filter off to the roundabout with the A4600, following the signs for City Centre. Cross the roundabout keeping along Ansty Road (A4600). It bears left, and you come to another roundabout. Take the right exit and continue for ¾ mile. Turn right into Swan Lane. Coventry City is ahead on the left.

From the **South & East:** Take the M1 to the M45 and follow onto the A45. At the roundabout junction with the A46, take the second exit keeping on the A45, and after 1.3 miles bear right onto the A444. Keep to the left past the roundabout on your right as you merge with London Road (A4114). Continue to the next roundabout and take the second exit going under the Ringway into White Friars Street, and then second right into Gosford Street. Pass back under the Ringway keeping left to come to the roundabout with Sky Blue Way. Take the right exit into Sky Blue Way, which runs into Walgrave Road. Swan Lane is the third turning on your left. Coventry City is ahead on the left.

Alternative route from the **South & East:** Take the A45 to the roundabout with the A46, and the third exit into London Road (B4110). Continue straight, over the next roundabout, keeping to the B4110 as it becomes Humber Road. Continue for 1½ miles until you reach Walgrave Road. Turn left and immediately right into Swan Lane. Coventry City is ahead on the left.

From the **North, South & West:** From the M6, exit at junction 2 onto the A4600. Then as from the North.

BY TRAIN

Coventry Railway Station (01203-832 304) is situated 1 mile from the ground.

BY BUS

From Poll Meadow Bus Station, Nos. 7, 17, 27, 32, 33.
From Trinity Street Bus Station, Nos. 35, 36.

IN THE AREA

RADIO
BBC Coventry & Warwickshire Radio - 94.8 FM & 103.7 FM: Fri 6 - 7pm, phone-in with guests from Coventry City; Sat 2 - 6pm, interview with players & managers, phone-in.

TOBY RESTAURANTS
Malt Shovel Toby Restaurant/Carving Room
Stonebridge Island, Nr. Meriden, Coventry CV7 7HL, tel: 01675-442 326.

Styvechale Arms
Kempas Highway, Coventry CV3 6PB, tel: 01203-410 199.

Craven
Brinklow Road, Coventry CV3 2DS, tel: 01203-458 456.

RESTAURANTS
Bourbons
American-style diner, from £5 per head, 100 Corporation Street, CV1 1EH, tel: 01203-550 145.

The Button Top Roast Inn
Great roasts, steaks, salmon, from £11 per head, 215 Beechwood Avenue, CV5 6HB, tel: 01203-714 332.

Macdonalds + drive-in
2 Wigston Road, CV2 2PZ, tel: 01203-612 492.

HOTELS / B&B
Forte Posthouse Coventry Hotel
147 ensuite rooms, all mod. cons. restaurant, bar, health club, children's play area, Hinkley Road, CV2 2HP, tel: 01203-613 261, from £57 per person per night, incl. services.

Brandon Hall Hotel
60 rooms, restaurant, bar, all mod. cons., Brandon, just outside Coventry, CV8 3FW, tel: 01203-542 571, rooms from £65 per night.

Fairlight Guest House
12 rooms, all mod. cons., 14 Regent Street, CV1 3EP, tel: 01203-224 215, from £15 per person per night.

PLACES TO VISIT
Heritage Motor Centre
Home of the largest collection of Bristol cars in the world, the Centre tells the history of the development of the British motor industry to the present day, Banbury Road, Gaydon, CV35 0BJ, tel: 01926-641 188, Open 7 days, 10am - 6pm, Adults £5.50, Juniors £3.50, U-5's free.

The Nickelodeon Line
A narrow gauge steam railway in a beautiful garden and woodland setting, plus mechanical instruments and organ, Ashorne Hill, CV33 9QN, tel: 01926-651 444, Open Sat. & Sun. afternoon, Adults £5.65, Juniors £3.25

Warwick Castle
An outstanding medieval castle, built by William the Conqueror, Warwick, CV34 4QU, tel: 01926-408 000, Open 7 days, Adults £8.25, Juniors £4.95.

Tourist Information Centre: 01203-832 304

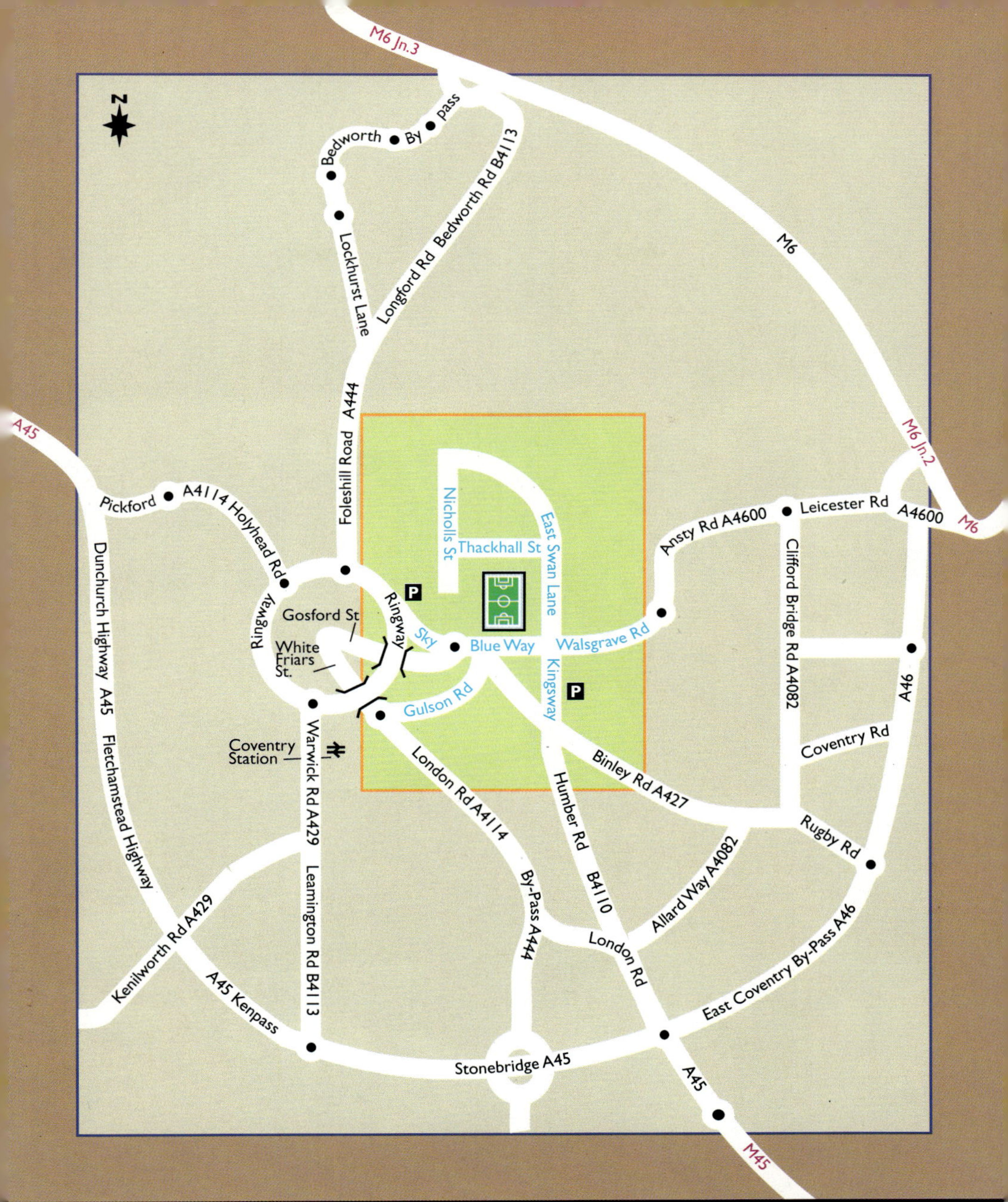

COVENTRY CITY FC

KICK OFF FM

Sports when you need it

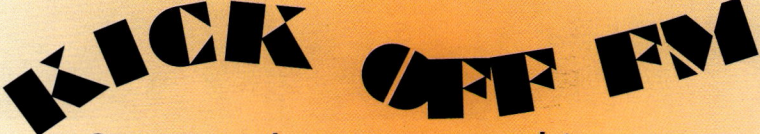

EVERTON FC

Club Number: 0151-330 2200
Tickets: 0151-330 2300
Club Call: 0891-12 11 99
Calls cost 39p/min. cheap, 49p/min. other times

Goodison Park
Goodison Road
Liverpool
Merseyside L4 4EL

Everton FC Shop
Goodison Park Stadium
Mon-Fri: 9am - 5pm
Sat/Sun Match Days: 9am - 3pm,
plus 4.30pm - 6pm
Match Eves: 9am - 7.30pm, 9pm - 10pm
Tel: 0151-330 2200, ext. 2030
Mail Order Tel: 0151-330 2333

The Everton Collection
Gwladys Street, Goodison Park
Match Days: 9am - 3pm, 4.30pm - 6pm
Match Eves: 4.30pm - 7.30pm, 9pm - 10pm
Mail Order Tel: 0151-330 2333

TICKETS

Booking Information
General Enquiries: 0151-330 2300
Recorded Information: 0891-12 15 99*
Credit Card Bookings: 0151-471 8000
Travel Club: 0151-330 2200, ext. 2218

Special Packages
Restaurant Facilities information: 0151-330 2499 or
0151-330 2200, ext. 2220

Stadium Tours, to be launched in August 1995

Corporate Hospitality & Sponsorship Packages,
Matchball, Individual & Kit Sponsorship:
0151-330 2400 or 0151-330 2200, ext. 2222

Match Day Prices Season 1995/96

	Cat. A	Cat. B
Main Stand		
Main Section	£17	£14
Top Balcony	£14 (£6)	£12 (£6)
Family Enclosure	£14 (£6)	£12 (£6)
Bullens Road Stand		
Upper Tier	£16	£14
Lower Tier	£14 (£6)	£12 (£6)
Paddock	£14	£12
Park Stand	£15	£13
Gwladys Stand		
Stand	£14	£12
Terrace	£12 (£6)	£10 (£6)
Visitors		
Upper	£16	£16
Lower	£16 (£10)	£16 (£10)

Prices in brackets denote Junior concessions.

STADIUM

Programme
£1.50

Official Magazine
Evertonian
£1

World Wide Fan Club
Contact the club for details: 0151-330 2200, ext. 2208

MAIN STAND
Seats 6,271
Blind facilities available
Ladbrokes
Snack Bars
Toilets

BULLENS STAND
Seats 5,726
First Aid Station
Ladbrokes
Snack Bars
Toilets

PARK STAND
Seats 5,888
Ladbrokes
Snack Bars
Programme Stand
Souvenir Shop
Toilets

GWLADYS STAND
Seats 7,892
Ladbrokes
Snack Bars
Programme Stand
Satellite Shop
Toilets

Disabled Access
Via Family Enclosure, Goodison Road,
50 Wheelchairs, 1 Helper per person

- VISITORS ENCLOSURE
- FAMILY ENCLOSURE
- DISABLED ENCLOSURE

BULLENS ROAD STAND
- Cat.A: £16/Cat.B: £14 — UPPER TIER
- Cat.A: £14(£6)/Cat.B: £12(£6) — LOWER TIER
- STAND TERRACE — Cat.A: £14/Cat.B: £12 — PADDOCK

GWLADYS STREET GWLADYS STAND
- Cat.A: £14 / Cat.A: £12(£6)
- Cat.B: £12 / Cat.B: £10(£6)

PARK STAND (GOODISON AVENUE)
- Cat.A: £15
- Cat B: £13

MAIN STAND (GOODISON ROAD)
- FAMILY ENCL.
- MAIN SECTION: Cat.A: £17/Cat.B: £14
- TOP BALCONY: Cat.A: £14(£6)/Cat.B: £12(£6)

EVERTON

GETTING TO THE GAME

Everton's Goodison Park is situated two miles north of Liverpool City Centre, opposite Stanley Park. Car parking is available in Anfield Road and sometimes in the streets adjacent to the stadium.

BY CAR

From the **North & South:** From the M6, exit at Junction 26 onto the M58 and continue until the end. At the gyratory, go left to join the M57 (Junction 7). Exit the M57 at Junction 4 to turn right into Lancashire Road (A580). Follow the road, across Queens Drive, into Walton Lane. Goodison Road is less than a mile along, on the right.

Alternative Route from **North**: From the M6, exit at Junction 26 onto the M58 and continue to the end. At the gyratory system, go a quarter way around, turning left onto the A59 Ormskirk Road. Continue along as the road becomes Rice Lane, and over the roundabout into County Road. Three quarters of a mile along County Road, turn left into Spellow Lane, and then left into Goodison Road. Goodison Park is on the right.

Alternative route from the **South**: From the M6, exit at Junction 21a onto the M62 to Liverpool. Follow to the end of the motorway and turn right onto the A5058 Queens Drive. After 4½ miles, at the roundabout junction with the A56, turn left into County Road. Three quarters of a mile along County Road, turn left into Spellow Lane, and then left into Goodison Road. Goodison Park is on the right.

From the **East**: From the M62, exit at Junction 6 onto the M57, signposted Southport, to Junction 7. Then same as for North.

From the **West**: From the M53, continue to Wallasey and follow to Liverpool via the Kingsway Mersey Tunnel. Turn left at the end into Scotland Road, taking the right fork to the A59 Kirkdale Road. Continue along as Kirkdale Road becomes Walton Road, for about ½ mile, and then turn right into Spellow Lane, and left into Goodison Road. Goodison Park is on the right.

BY TRAIN

Lime Street Railway Station: (0151-709 9696) is in the town centre, 2 miles from Goodison Park
Kirkdale Railway Station is 10 mins. walk from the ground, in Westminster Road.

BY BUS

Bus depot is situated in front of the Railway Station.
Bus Information, tel: 0151-236 7676
Stand L, Bus 17 and 217, every 10 minutes.

IN THE AREA

RADIO

City FM Sport - 96.7FM, 1548 AM: Sat 2pm - 6pm, round-up of all premiership matches and live commentaries of local team matches. Pre-game and post-game views and discussion.
BBC Radio Merseyside - 95.8 FM, 1485 AM: Sat 2pm - 6pm & Fri 7pm - 10pm, in-depth match news and views.

TOBY RESTAURANTS

Greenhills Toby Restaurant
Booker Avenue, Mossley Hill, Liverpool, L18 5TN, tel: 0151-724 1101.

Greave Dunning
Greasby Road, Greasby, Merseyside L49 3NX, tel: 0151-678 4509.

Hotel Victoria
Lower Village, Heswall, Wirral, Merseyside L60 8QE, tel: 0151-342 6021.

RESTAURANTS

El Macho
Traditional Mexican, From £15 per head, 23 Hope Street, L1 9BQ, tel: 0151-708 6644.

Lux Garden
Chinese cuisine, lunch £4.80 incl.wine, dinner £17.50 per head, 204-206 Warbeck Moor, L9 0HZ, tel: 0151-530 1499

L'Allouette
French cuisine, from £15 per head, 2 Park Lane, L17 8US, tel: 0151-727 2142.

HOTELS / B&B

Holiday Inn
83 ensuite rooms, restaurant, bar, free parking, leisure club, Centre Island, Lower Mersey Street, Waterways, Ellesmere Port, South Wirral, L65 2AL, tel: 0151-356 8111, from £50 per double room.

The Haydock Thistle Hotel
139 ensuite rooms, all mod. cons., Penny Lane, Haydock, WA11 9SG, tel: 01942-272 000, rooms from £79.

The Antrim Hotel
Family run, 20 rooms, all mod. cons., 73 Mount Pleasant, L3 5TB, tel: 0151-709 5239, rooms from £24.

Lake View
5 rooms, overlooking gardens and river, 19 Adelaide Terrace, L22 8QD, tel: 0151-920 9754, from £35 per double room.

PLACES TO VISIT

Liverpool Museum & Planetarium
From the Amazon to Outer Space, William Brown Street, L3 8EN, tel: 0151-207 0001, Open Mon-Sat: 10am - 5pm; Sun: 12 - 5pm

Seacombe Submarine Aquarium
Giant rays, octopus, sharks and the scary conger eel, plus wave machine, Victoria Place, Seacombe, L44 6QY, tel: 0151-630 1030, Open daily from 10am, Adults £1.50, Juniors 70p.

Tourist Information Centre: 0151-709 3631

EVERTON FC

tune into that **big match** *atmosphere* — THE NORTH WEST SPORTS LEADER — 96.7 City FM — LIVE COMMENTARY

HOME OR AWAY

THISTLE HOTELS
PREMIER STYLE IN PREMIER LOCATIONS.

FOR FURTHER DETAILS CONTACT
THISTLE HOTELS
2 THE CALLS, LEEDS LS2 7JU
TEL: 0113 243 9111

LEEDS UNITED AFC

Club Number: 0113-271 6037
Tickets: 0113-271 0710
Club Call: 0891-12 11 80
*Calls cost 39p/min. cheap, 49p/min. other times

Elland Road
Leeds
LS11 0ES

Leeds United Collection
1: 10/11 Burton's Arcade, Leeds
2: 16 Little Westgate, Wakefield
Both shops are open
Mon-Sat: 9.30am - 5.15pm

There are 5 other Match Day Shops located at various points around the stadium.

Leeds United Souvenir Shop
Elland Road Stadium
Mon-Fri: 9am - 5pm
Sat. Match Days: 9am - kickoff, plus 30 mins. after the game
Sun. Match Days: 9am - kickoff, plus 30 mins. after the game
Match Eves: 9am - kickoff, plus 30 mins. after the game
Tel: 0113-270 6844
Fax: 0113-270 6560
Mail Order Service:
Tel: 0113-270 3077

TICKETS

Booking Information
General Enquiries: 0113-271 6037
Recorded Information: 0891-12 16 80*
Credit Card Bookings: 0113-271 0710
Travel Club: 0113-271 6037

Special Packages
Restaurant Facilities:
For Matchday Enquiries and for information on Midweek Conferences and Seminars, contact Banqueting: 0113-272 0492
Stadium Tours, contact Dick Wright: 0113-271 6037
Corporate Hospitality & Sponsorship Packages, contact the Commercial Office: 0113-271 0168

Match Day Prices Season 1995/96

	A+	A	B	C
West Stand				
Upper Tier & Paddock	£25	£22	£21	£20
Stand B	£19	£16	£15	£14
Revie Stand	£19	£16	£15	£14
East Stand				
Upper Tier	£23	£20	£19	£18
Family Stand	£21	£18	£17	£16
South Stand				
Upper & Lower Tiers	£19	£16	£15	£14
North East Stand & North West Stand	£21	£18	£17	£16

STADIUM

Programme £1.50
Subscription available
Official Monthly Magazine
Leeds United Magazine £2
Fanzines
Marching Altogether 50p
The Hanging Sheep 60p
The Square Ball £1

Disabled Access
West Stand: 40 Chairs;
Revie Stand: 25 Chairs;
South West Corner: 34 Chairs

WEST STAND
Seats 7,306
Fast Food
Ladbrokes

REVIE STAND
Seats 6,899
Fast Food
Ladbrokes
2 Licensed Lounge Areas
Souvenir Shop

EAST STAND
Seats 6,010
Fast Food
Ladbrokes
Souvenir Shop

FAMILY STAND
Seats 8,710
Amusement-Arcade
Fast Food/Shopping-Concourse
Ladbrokes
2 Souvenir Shops
Video Wall

SOUTH STAND
Seats 3,907
Fast Food
Ladbrokes

NORTH EAST STAND
Seats 2,685
Fast Food
Ladbrokes

NORTH WEST STAND
Seats 476
Fast Food

SOUTH EAST STAND
Seats 1,837
Fast Food

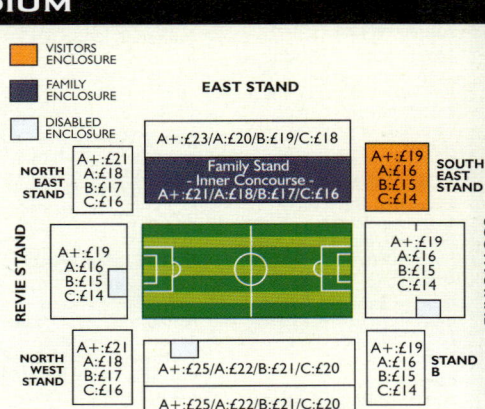

Getting to the Game

Leeds United football ground is situated two miles south-west of the city centre. The redevelopment of the stadium is now complete, offering many excellent new facilities. There are two car parks adjacent to the ground. The streets opposite Elland Road - in the vicinity of Heath Grove - are mostly restricted to residential permit holders, but further on some unrestricted spaces can be found.

By Car

From the **North:** Take the A61 into the City centre. At Hunslet Road, turn right and follow signs for the M621. Take the M621 West for 1½ miles to the Junction 2 roundabout and turn left into the the A643 Elland Road. The ground is on the right.

From the **North-East:** Take the A64 (or the A63 which joins the A64) York Road into the City Centre. Turn left at Marsh Lane to join the A61. Then same as for North.

From the **East:** Take the M62 to Junction 29 and then the M1 to the City centre. Keep to the left and join the M621. Turn left at the first junction with the A643, Elland Road. The ground is on the right.

From the **South:** Take the M1 to the City centre. Then same as for the East.

From the **West:** From the M62, exit at Junction 27 and then take the M621 for 3½ miles until Junction 2. Turn left at the roundabout onto the A643 Elland Road. The ground is on the right.

By Train

Leeds Railway Station: 0113-244 8133

By Bus

93 and 96 to Beeston from City Square, every 10 minutes. Special Match Day buses run regularly from Sovereign Street.

Coach parking as directed by police.

In The Area

Radio

BBC Radio Leeds - 92.4 FM, 774 MW: Sat 1pm - 6pm, live commentary from Leeds, following local clubs, interviews with players & managers, full results service.

Magic 828 - 828 AM: Sat 2pm - 6pm, pre-match build-up and full Leeds match coverage, plus roundup of premiership games.

Toby Restaurants

Eleventh Earl Toby Carving Room
Fink Hill, Horsforth, Leeds LS18 4DW, tel: 0113-258 6401.

Bridge Inn
Walshford, nr. Wetherby, LS22 5HS, tel: 01937-580 115.

Grove
Aberford Road, Oulton, Leeds LS26 8EJ, tel: 0113-282 6201.

Restaurants

Brasserie 44
Elegant bistro, £25 p.p. 42-44 The Calls, Leeds L52 7AW, 0113-234 3232

The Italian Job
Authentic Italian, £15 p.p. 9 Bride End Lower Briggate, LS2 7EW, tel: 0113-242 0185.

Harry Ramsden's
Famous fish & chips, £8 p.p. Larwood House White Cross, Guisely, LS20 8LZ, tel: 01943-874 641.

Hotels / B&B

Holiday Inn
125 ensuite rooms, restaurant, bars, health suite, free parking, Wellington Street, Leeds LS1 4DL, tel: 0113-244 2200, from £72 per double room, incl. breakfast.

The Thistle Merrion Hotel
The Merrion Centre, Wade Lane, LS2 8NH, tel: 0113-243 9191, Singles £39.50, Doubles £57.50.

City Centre Hotel
51a New Briggate, LS2 8JD, tel: 0113-242 9019, Singles £20, Doubles £40.

Crescent Private Hotel
274 Dewsbury Road, Beeston, LS11 6JT, tel: 0113-270 1819, Singles £16, Doubles £32.

Places To Visit

Tetleys Brewery Wharf
The story of english pubs, past present & future: Adults £4.50, Juniors £2.50, £3.60 Conc. Family ticket - 2A+3J - £12. The Waterfront, LS1 1QG, tel: 0113-242 0666, Tue-Sun 10.30am - 4pm (last tour).

Tropical World
All year round tropical paradise. Admission Free. Canal Gardens, Roundhay Park, LS8 2ER, tel: 0113-266 1850

Granary Wharf
Friendly, interesting shopping and entertainment centre, The Canal Basin, LS1 4BR, tel: 0113-244 6570

Leeds City Museum
Temple, Jungle, hands-on exhibits
The Headrow, Leeds LS1 3AA, Free Admission, tel: 0113-247 8275

Thwaite Mills
Island out-of-time guide tour, located off the A61, Thwaite Lane, Stourton, LS10 1RP, tel: 0113-249 6453, Adults £2.00, Conc. £1.00, Juniors 50p.

Tourist Information:
tel: 0113-247 8392

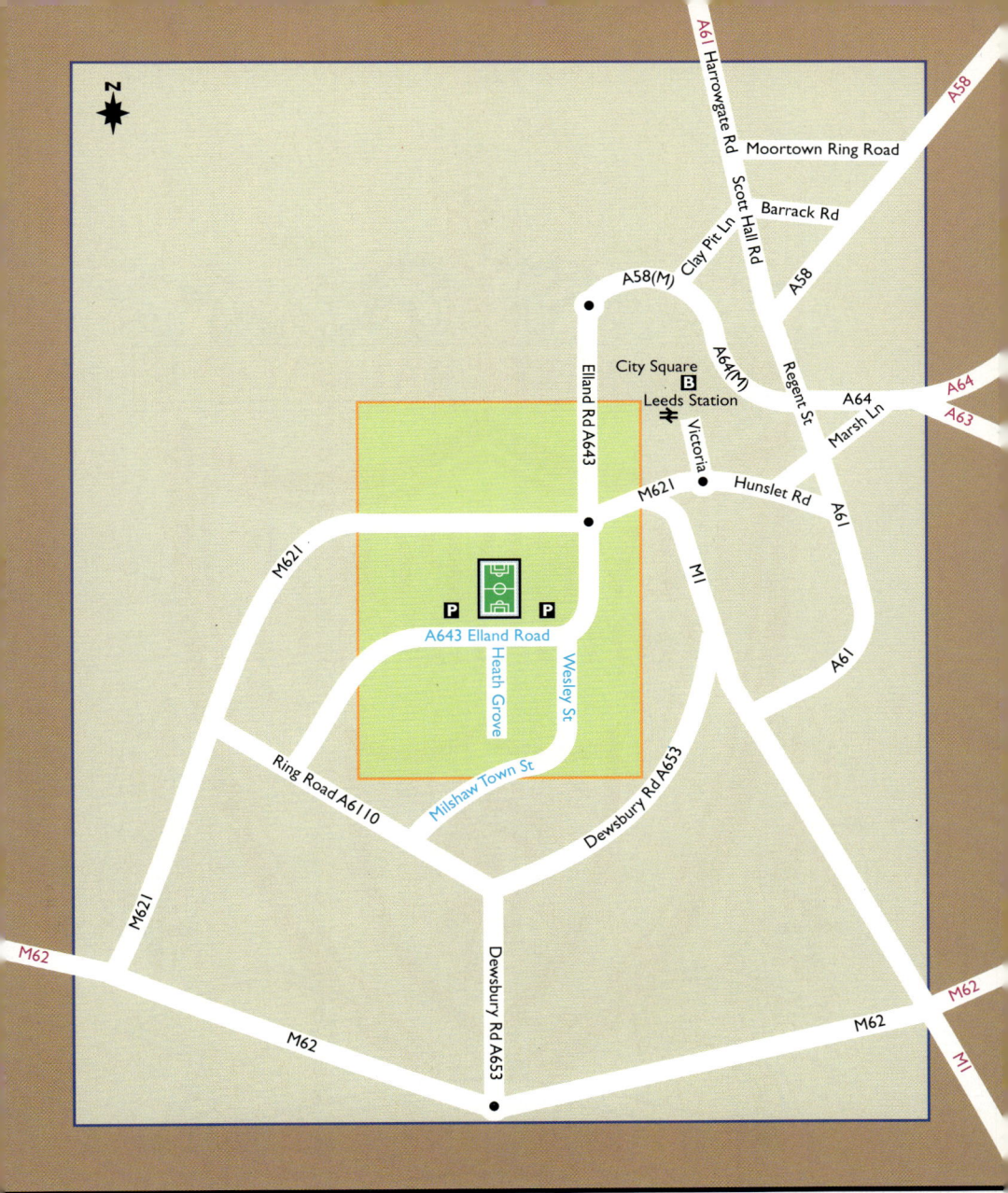

LEEDS UNITED AFC

BBC RADIO LEEDS
Another Premier Team

92.4FM 774MW

YOU'LL NEVER WALK ALONE

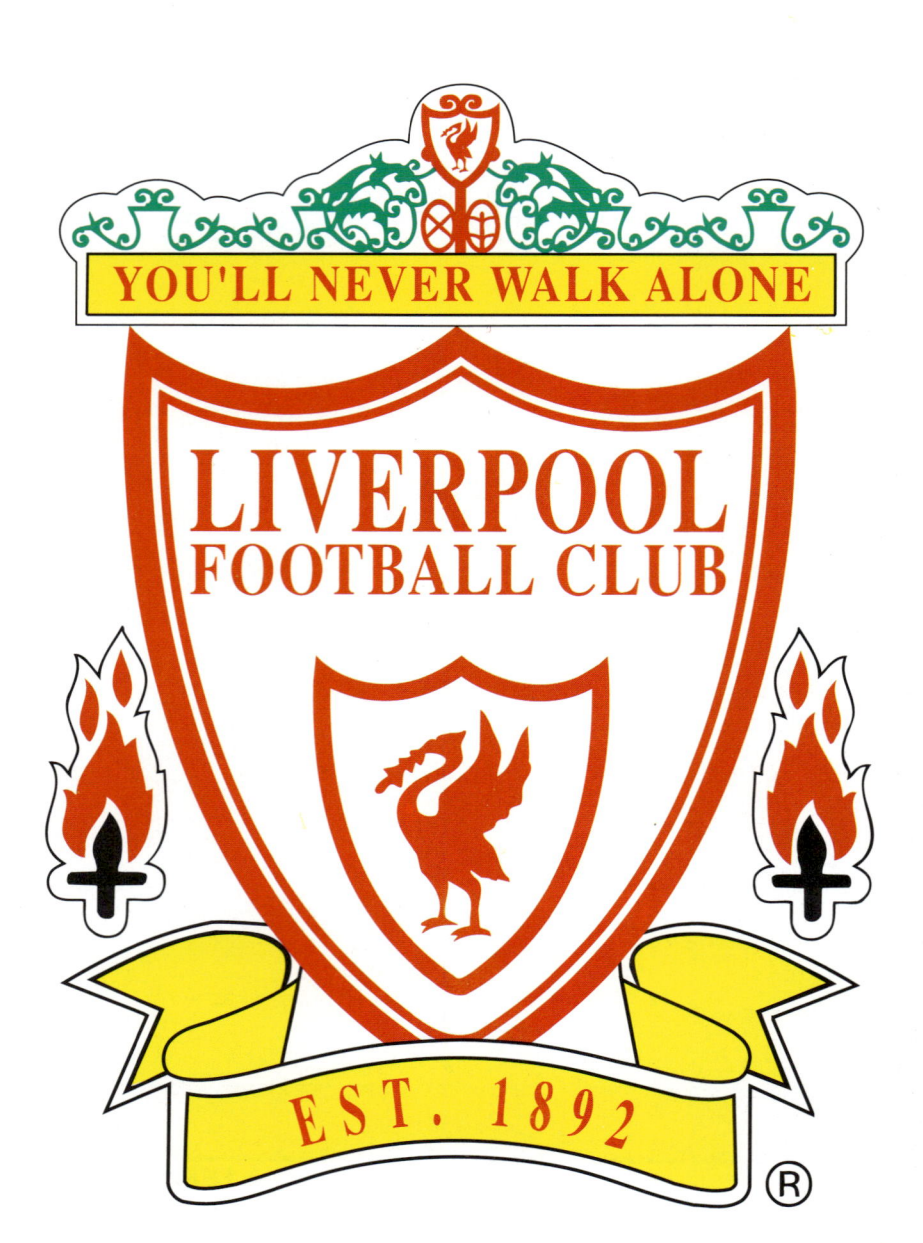

LIVERPOOL
FOOTBALL CLUB

EST. 1892

LIVERPOOL FC

Club Number: 0151-263 2361
Tickets: 0151-260 8680
Club Call: 0891-12 11 84
*Calls cost 39p/min. cheap, 49p/min. other times

LFC REDS

Anfield Road
Liverpool
Merseyside
L4 0TH

LFC Club Shop
Kop Grandstand
Mon-Fri: 9am - 5pm
Sat. Match Days: 9am - 6pm
Sun. Match Days: 9am - 6pm
Match Eves: 9am - 9.30pm
Tel: 0151-263 1760
Fax:: 0151-260 8813
<u>Mail Order Service:</u>
Tel: 0151-260 1515

TICKETS

Booking Information
General Enquiries: 0151-260 8680
Recorded Information: 0151-260 9999
Credit Card Bookings: 0151-263 5727
Travel Club: 0151-263 2361

Special Packages
Conference, Banqueting & Restaurant Facilities, contact Simon Pile: 0151-263 7744
Stadium Tours, contact Brian Hall: 0151-260 1433
Corporate Hospitality & Sponsorship Packages, contact Commercial Department: 0151-263 9199

Match Day Prices Season 1995/96

	Premium	Standard
Main Stand	£16	£15
Paddock Enclosure	£16	£15
Centenary Stand		
Upper Tier	£16	£15
Lower Tier	£16	£15
Anfield Road Stand	£16	£15
Family Ticket: 1 Adult+1 Child	£24	£22.50
Kop Grandstand	£13	£12
Family Ticket: 1 Adult+1 Child	£19.50	£18

STADIUM

Programme £1.50
Official Magazine £1.95

MAIN STAND
Seats 8,909
Ladbrokes
Licensed Bars
Snack Bars
Toilets

PADDOCK ENCLOSURE
Seats 2,640
Licensed Bar
Snack Bars
Toilets

CENTENARY STAND
Seats 11,410
Ladbrokes
Licensed Bars
Snack Bars
Toilets

ANFIELD ROAD STAND
Seats 5,512
Ladbrokes
Snack Bars
Toilets

KOP GRANDSTAND
Seats 12,199
Fast Food
Ladbrokes
Licensed Bars
Snack Bars
Toilets

Disabled Access
Kop Grandstand: 60 Wheelchairs, 1 Helper per person

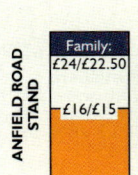

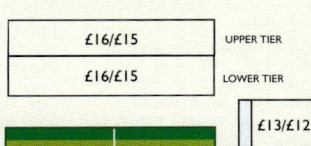

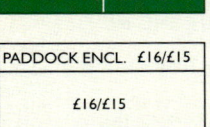

VISITORS ENCLOSURE
FAMILY ENCLOSURE
DISABLED ENCLOSURE

CENTENARY STAND
£16/£15 UPPER TIER
£16/£15 LOWER TIER

ANFIELD ROAD STAND
Family: £24/£22.50
£16/£15

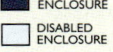

WALTON BRECK ROAD
KOP STAND
£13/£12
Family: £19.50/£18

PADDOCK ENCL. £16/£15
£16/£15
MAIN STAND

LIVERPOOL

GETTING TO THE GAME

Liverpool's Anfield Road Ground is situated two miles north of Liverpool City Centre, across from Stanley Park. There is a sizeable car park by the Sports Centre in the park. This fills up quickly, the earlier you arrive the surer you will be to find a space.

BY CAR

From the **North & South:** From the M6, exit at Junction 26 onto the M58 and continue until the end. At the gyratory, go left to join the M57 (Junction 7). Exit the M57 at Junction 4 to turn right into Lancashire Road (A580). Follow all the way, across Queens Drive, into Walton Lane. Anfield Road is on the left, at the end of Stanley Park.

Alternative Route from **North**: From the M6, exit at Junction 26 onto the M58 and continue to the end. At the gyratory system, go a quarter way around, turning left onto the A59 Ormskirk Road. Continue along as the road becomes Rice Lane. Watch for signs to Walton Hall Avenue, and at the roundabout turn left into Queens Drive Road (A5058) and right into Walton Hall Avenue, which becomes Walton Lane. At the end of Stanley Park, turn left into Anfield Road. The ground is on the right.

Alternative route from the **South:** From the M6, exit at Junction 21a onto the M62 to Liverpool. Follow to the end of the motorway and turn right onto the A5058 Queens Drive. After 3 miles, turn left into Utting Avenue, which becomes Arkles Lane. At the end of Stanley Park, turn right into Anfield Road. The ground is on the left.

From the **East:** From the M62, exit at junction 6 onto the M57 to Junction 7. Then same as for the North.

From the **West:** From the M53, continue to Wallasey and follow to Liverpool via the Kingsway Mersey Tunnel. Turn left at the end into Scotland Road, taking the right fork to the A59 Kirkdale Road. Turn right into Everton Valley and Walton Breck Road. The ground is on the left.

BY TRAIN

Lime Street Railway Station: (0151-709 9696) is in the town centre, 2 miles from Anfield Road. Kirkdale Railway Station is 10 mins. walk from the ground, in Westminster Road.

BY BUS

Bus depot is situated in front of the Railway Station.
Bus Information, tel: 0151-236 7676
Stand L, Bus 17 and 217, direct to Anfield, every 10 minutes.

IN THE AREA

RADIO
City FM Sport - 96.7FM, 1548 AM: Sat 2pm - 6pm, round-up of all premiership matches and live commentaries of local team matches. Pre-game and post-game views and discussion.

BBC Radio Merseyside - 95.8 FM, 1485 AM: Sat 2pm - 6pm & Fri 7pm - 10pm, in-depth match news and views.

TOBY RESTAURANTS
Halfway House Toby Restaurant
Woolton Road, Childwall, Liverpool L16 8NE, tel: 0151-722 1132.

Bay Horse Toby Restaurant
Church Road, Formby, Liverpool L37 8BQ, tel: 01704-873 890.

The Merebrook
Allport Road, Bromborough, Wirral, Merseyside L62 2DD, tel: 0151-334 0037.

RESTAURANTS
The Armadillo
£25 p.p., 31 Mathew St., LS2, tel: 0151-236 4123

Mayflower
Authentic Chinese, £15 p.p., 48 Duke St., L1 5AF, tel: 0151 709 6339

Harry Ramsdens
Famous fish and chips, £8 p.p., Brunswick Way, Sefton St. L3 4BN, tel: 0151 709 4545

HOTELS / B&B
Holiday Inn
83 ensuite rooms, restaurant, bar, free parking, leisure club, Centre Island, Lower Mersey Street, Waterways, Ellesmere Port, South Wirral, L65 2AL, tel: 0151-356 8111, from £50 per double room.

The Atlantic Tower Thistle
Waterfront views, nr. Albert Docks, 226 en-suite rooms, Single £85, Double £99, Chapel Street, L3 9RE, tel: 0151-227 4444

Tina's
Guesthouse by the ground, 16 rooms, Single £15, Double £30, 71 Anfield Road, Anfield, L4 0TQ, tel: 0151-263 9400

PLACES TO VISIT
The Beatles Story
Experience the magic of the Cavern Club, at the Brittania Vaults, Albert Dock, Liverpool L3 4AA, tel: 0151-709 1963. Adults £5.45, Juniors/Conc. £3.95, Open 7 Days, 10am - 6pm..

Pleasure Island
World's largest indoor play area, plus nature reserve, crazy golf, bowling, rollerskating. International Festival Park, Riverside Drive, Otters Pool, Liverpool L17 7HJ, tel: 0151-728 7766, £6.95 Adult, £5.95 Juniors/Conc.

Merseyside Maritime Museum
Five floors of interest, Albert Dock, Liverpool L3 4AQ, tel: 0151-207 0001, Adults £3, Juniors/Conc. £1.50, Open 7 Days, 10.30am - 5.30pm (last admission 4.30pm).

Tourist Information Centre: 0151-709 3631

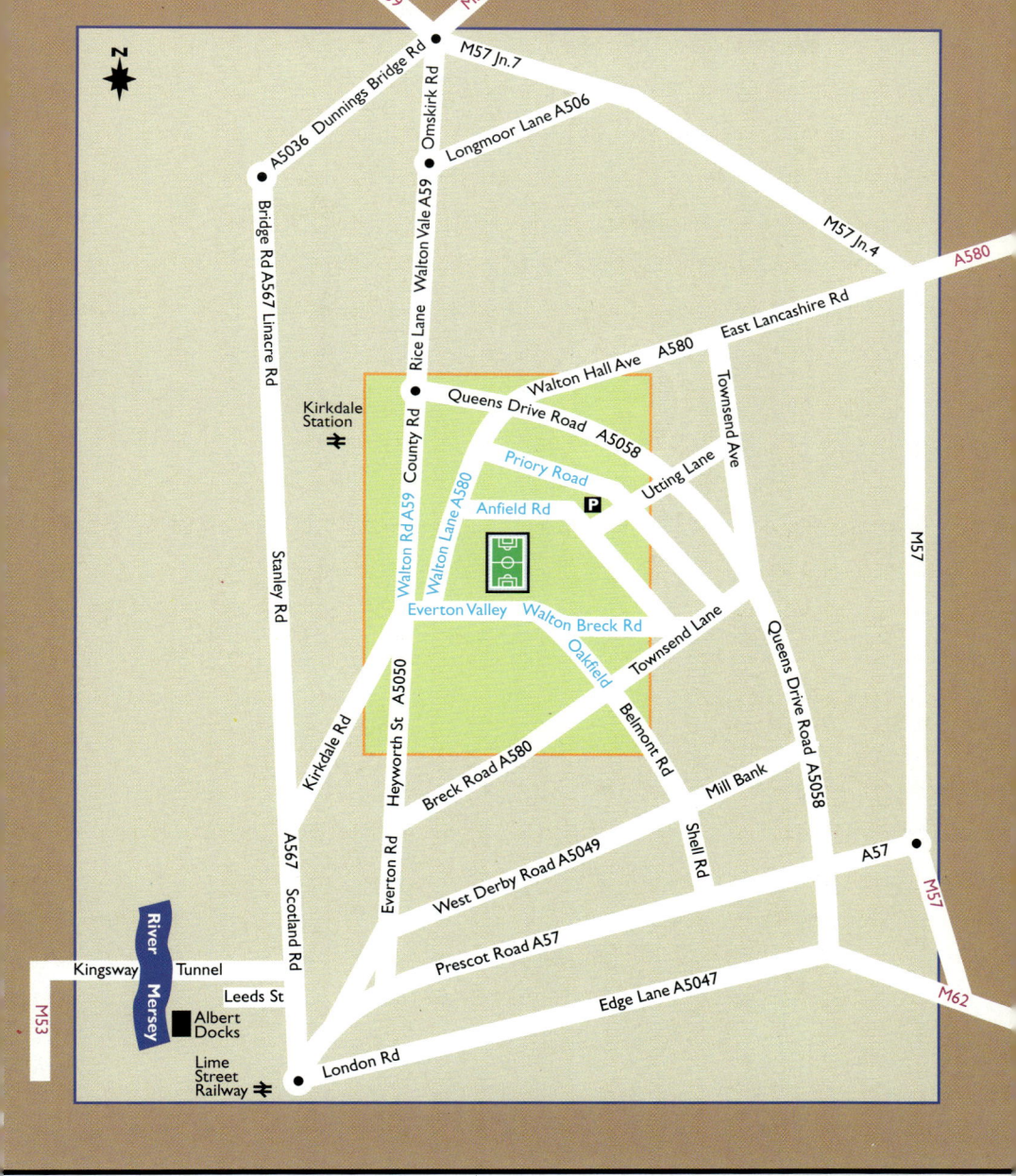

LIVERPOOL FC

tune into that big match atmosphere

THE NORTH WEST SPORTS LEADER

96.7 City FM

brother®

We're City's greatest supporter.

LASER PRINTERS · FAX MACHINES · TYPEWRITERS · WORD PROCESSORS · LABELLING MACHINES
DOMESTIC AND INDUSTRIAL SEWING MACHINES · KNITTING MACHINES

Brother International Europe Ltd., Brother House, 1 Tame Street, Audenshaw, Manchester, M34 5JE.

MANCHESTER CITY FC

Club Number: 0161-224 5000
Tickets: 0161-226 2224
Club Call: 0891-12 11 91
*Calls cost 39p/min. cheap, 49p/min. other times

Maine Road
Moss Side
Manchester
M14 7WN

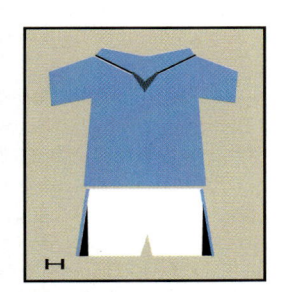

Manchester City F.C. Souvenir Shop
Maine Road Stadium
Mon-Fri: 9.30am - 5pm
Sat. Match Days: 9.30am - kickoff,
plus 30 mins. after the game
Sun. Match Days: 9.30am - kickoff,
plus 30 mins. after the game
Match Eves: 9.30am - kickoff,
plus 30 mins. after the game
Tel: 0161-226 4824
Fax: 0161-226 7128

Manchester City F.C. Souvenir Shop
Kippax Stand
Open Match Days only

TICKETS

Booking Information
General Enquiries: 0161-226 2224
Credit Card Bookings: 0161-227 9229
Travel Club: 0161-226 5047

Special Packages
Restaurant Facilities, contact Geoff Durbin
in the Commercial Office: 0161-248 9999

Stadium Tours, contact Community Officer
Alex Williams: 0161-226 1782

Corporate Hospitality & Sponsorship Packages,
Matchday & Matchball Sponsorship,
Club Patron packages
contact Geoff Durbin: 0161-248 9999

Match Day Prices Season 1995/96

Main Stand
Blocks B,C	£16
Other Blocks	£15
Block G (Sen.Cit. only)	£5

North Stand
Adults	£10
Juv., Sen.Cit.	£7
BLocks K,L (Juv./Sen.Cit.)	£5

Umbro Stand
Main Section	£11
JD Sports Family Encl. Adults	£8
JD Sports Family Encl. Juv/Sen.Cit.	£5

Kippax Stand
Upper Tier	£14
Lower Tier	£11

Any obstructed views: £2 reduction
All prices subject to a £1 alteration dependent on match

STADIUM

Programme £1.50
Official Magazine £1.95
Fanzines
Blue Print £1
Electric Blue £1
King of the Kippax £1.25
This Charming Fan 50p

MAIN STAND
Seats 8,084
Ladbrokes
Licensed Bar
Restaurants
Snack Bar
Toilets

NORTH STAND
Seats 7,448
Family Area
Ladbrokes
Licensed Bar
Snack Bar
Toilets

KIPPAX STAND
Seats 9,742
Fast Food
Ladbrokes
Licensed Bar
Restaurants
Souvenir Shop
(Match Days only)

UMBRO STAND
Seats 4,541
Family Stand
Fast Food
Licensed Bar
Toilets

Disabled Access
Umbro & Kippax Stands: 79 Wheelchairs, 1 Helper per person

MANCHESTER CITY

GETTING TO THE GAME

Manchester City's Maine Road ground is situated a mile and a half south of the city centre. Local parking restrictions can be fierce, and it is advisable to take care when locking up the car. The club occasionally sets up temporary car parks, and some of the local schools are amenable to drivers parking in their grounds. Otherwise, use one of the many car parks in town and bus in.

By Car

From the **North**: From the M61, turn onto the M62 westbound to join the M63. Exit the M63 at Junction 9, following signs to Manchester along the A5103 Princess Road. 3 miles on, turn right into Claremont Road. A third of a mile on, turn right into Maine Road.

From the **South**: From the M6, exit at Junction 19 onto the A556 to Stockport, to join the M56 Eastbound. Continue straight at Junction 3 into the A5103 Princess Parkway, which becomes Princess Park Road, to Manchester. After 3 miles, turn right into Claremont Road, and then after a third of a mile turn right into Maine Road.

From the **East**: From the M62, keep to the left hand lane past Worsley and join the M602 Salford Motorway, and continue to the end. Keeping right, follow straight onto the A57 Regent Road. Passing under the railway bridge, head onto the Mancunian Way (A57M). At the flyover, bear left and follow signposts to Moss Side, along the slip road. At the island turn right into Princess Road. After 1½ miles, turn left into Claremont Road, and then after a third of a mile turn right into Maine Road.

From the **West**: From M62, join M63 at Junction 12. Exit the M63 at Junction 9. Then same as for the North.
Or, From M56, follow to Junction 3, continue straight into Princess Parkway, which becomes Princess Park Road. After 3 miles, turn right into Claremont Road, and then after a third of a mile turn right into Maine Road.

Alternative route through **City Centre** for **North** and **East**: Exit M62 at Junction 17 onto the A56 Bury Road, following signs to 'Airport'. Continue along through the city. After the Bridgewater Viaduct, turn left onto the Mancunian Way (A57M). At the flyover, bear left and follow signposts to Moss Side, along the slip road. At the island turn right into Princess Road. After 1½ miles, turn left into Claremont Road, and then after a third of a mile turn right into Maine Road.

By Train

Railway Information: 0161-832 8353. From Piccadilly Station you can catch the Metro train system straight to the ground - Old Trafford Metro Station.

By Bus

Bus Information: 0161-228 7811
From Piccadilly Square, nos. 3, 4, 5, 6, 252, 257, 263.

IN THE AREA

RADIO

Piccadilly Gold Sport - 103 FM, 1152 AM: Sat 1 - 6pm, pre-match and after-match phone-in, plus live commentaries of top local games. Also Sunday pm if Premier League match on.

GMR - 95.1 FM: 2 - 6pm Sat., reporting live from local big games; also 2.30 - 6pm Sun., 7 - 10pm Tue, Wed., if match on, and hourly sports report.

TOBY RESTAURANTS

Cherrys
Harden Park, Alderley Edge, Cheshire, Greater Manchester SK9 7QN, tel: 01625-582 294.

Owl and Spindle Toby Restaurant
Burnley Lane, Chadderton, Oldham, Greater Manchester OL1 2QS, tel: 0161-627 3883.

Pier 6 Toby Restaurant
Clipper Quay, Salford Quays, Manchester M5 2XP, tel: 0161-872 9989.

RESTAURANTS

Harry Ramsden's
Great fish and chips, from £6 per head, 1 Water Street, M3 4JU, tel: 0161-832 9144.

Golden Rice Bowl
Chinese cuisine, from £20 per head, 33a Cross Street, M2 1ML, tel: 0161-832 9033.

Guilios Terrazza
Italian cuisine, from £25 per head, 14 Nicolas Street, M1 4EJ, tel: 0161-236 4033.

HOTELS / B&B

Holiday Inn
303 ensuite rooms, restaurants, bars, indoor pool, Crowne Plaza, Peter Street, Manchester M60 2DS, tel: 0161-228 2241, from £96 per double room, incl. breakfast.

The Portland Thistle Hotel
205 ensuite rooms, restaurant, bar, indoor pool, Portland Street, Piccadilly Gardens, M1 6DP, tel: 0161-228 3400, from £92.

Monroes Hotel
7 ensuite rooms, all mod. cons., restaurant, bar, 38 London Road, M1 1PE, tel: 0161-263 0564, from £22.

Tourist Information Centre: 0161-234 3157

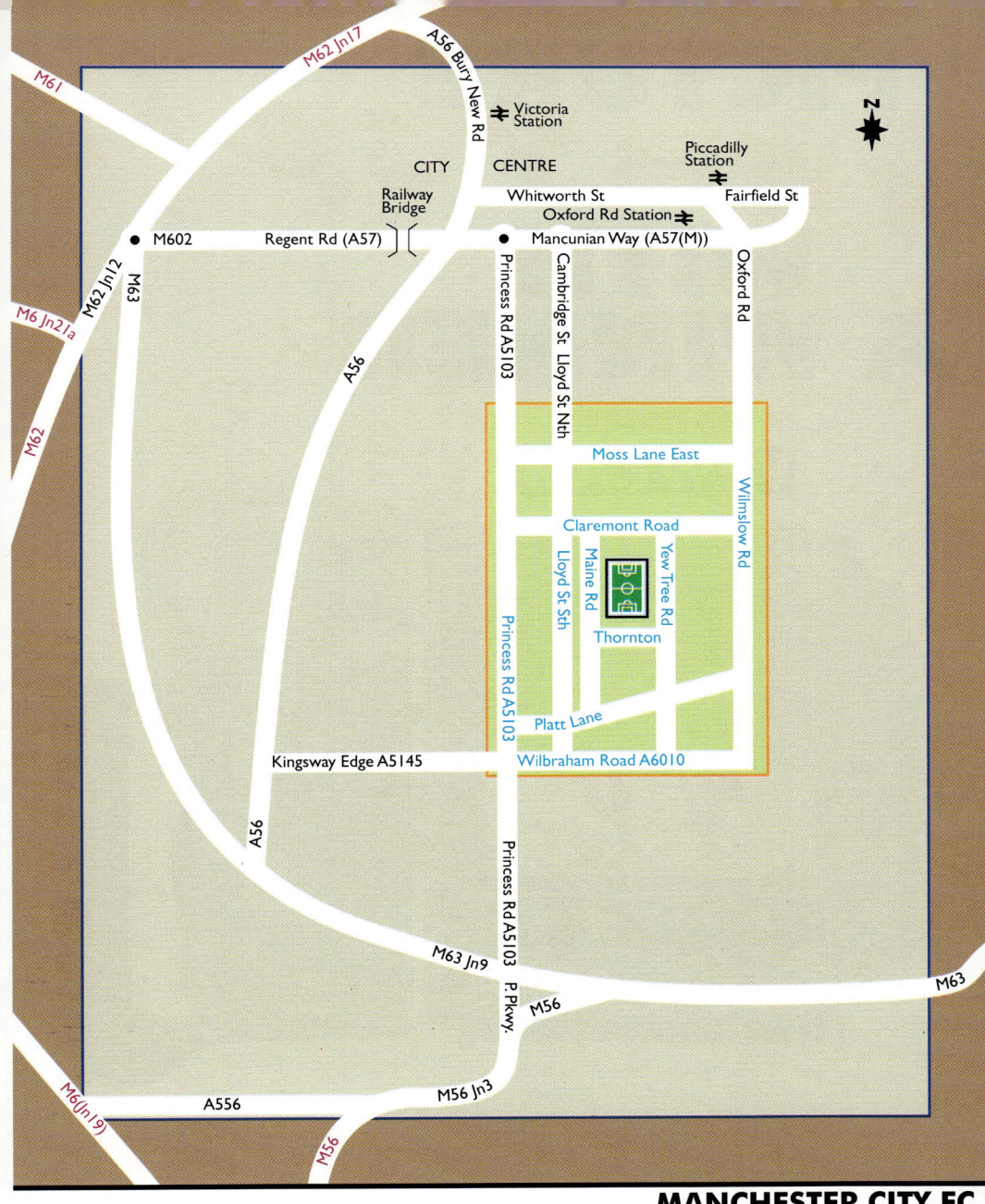

MANCHESTER CITY FC

For full match commentary

PICCADILLY RADIO 1152 AM

Always number one for sport

PICTURE *yourself* WITH A WINNER

SHARP
VIEW·CAM

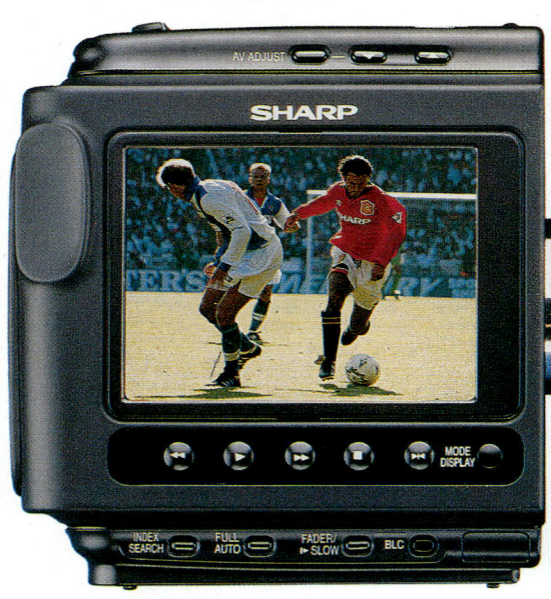

Sharp's latest winner is the revolutionary new **VIEWCAM** – the world's first fully integrated video camera, 8mm video deck and LCD colour monitor!

The **SHARP VIEWCAM** features a winning line-up of easy to use star attractions, for example, the LCD colour monitor means the end of "squinting" down a tiny viewfinder – you simply frame the subject or scene and press record!

The pivot between monitor and lens on the other hand offers total flexibility allowing low or high angle shots from almost any position. Swing the lens through 180 degrees to face the same way as the monitor and the **SHARP VIEWCAM** even lets you record yourself!

Replaying your action couldn't be easier either, as the LCD colour monitor delivers instant video playback with sound from the built in speaker – so family and friends can gather round and immediately share the fun.

SHARP
INTELLIGENT THINKING

SHARP ELECTRONICS (UK) LTD, SHARP HOUSE, THORP ROAD, NEWTON HEATH, MANCHESTER M40 5BE
For further information please call FREEPHONE 0800 262958

SHARP • **VIEW·CAM** • TV • VIDEO • AUDIO • MICROWAVE OVEN • COPIER • FAX • CALCULATOR • ELECTRONIC TYPEWRITER • ELECTRONIC IQ ORGANISER • NOTEBOOK PC • ELECTRONIC CASH REGISTER

MANCHESTER UNITED FC

MUFC RED DEVILS

Club Number: 0161-872 1661
Tickets: 0161-872 0199
Club Call: 0891-12 11 61
Calls cost 39p/min. cheap, 49p/min. other times

Old Trafford Stadium
Sir Matt Busby Way
Old Trafford
Manchester M16 0RA

Megastore
21-26 United Road,
Mon-Sat: 9am - 5pm
Sun: 10am - 4pm
Sat. Match Days: 9am - 3pm,
Sun. Match Days: 10am - kickoff,
plus 1 hour after the game
Match Eves: 9am - kickoff,
plus 1 hour after the game
Tel: 01161-848 8181

Superstore
Old Trafford
Tue-Fri: 9am - 5pm, Sat: 9am - 4pm
Sat. Match Days: 9am - 3pm,
plus 1 hour after game
Sun. Match Days: 9.30am - kickoff,
plus 1 hour after game
Match Eves: 9am - kickoff,
plus 1 hour after game
Tel: 0161-872 3398,
Fax: 0161-877 6381

Manchester United FC Museum
Open Tues-Sun: 10am - 4pm
Adults: £2.95, Conc.: £1.95
Family Ticket: £6.95
Stadium Tour plus Museum:
Adults: £4.95, Conc.: £2.95

Mail Order Service
For both shops
Tel: 0161-877 9777,
Fax: 0161-872 0941

TICKETS

Booking Information
General Enquiries: 0161-872 1661
Club General Enquiries: 0161-930 1968
General Enquiries Fax: 0161-876 5502
Recorded Information: 0161-872 0199
Travel Club: 0161-872 5208

Special Packages
Executive Suite Restaurant: 0161-872 3331
Stadium Tours on Tue-Sun: 10am - 4pm:
0161-877 4002
Corporate Hospitality & Sponsorship Packages,
contact Commercial Department: 0161-872 3488
Membership Office: 0161-872 5208

Match Day Prices Season 1995/96

Due to major rebuilding throughout 1995/96 there will be no matchday tickets available - at least during the early part of the season. Further information will be announced when it becomes available.

STADIUM

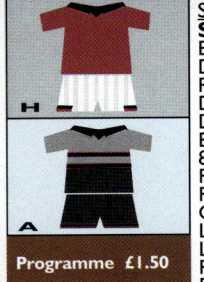

Programme £1.50
Official Magazine
Manchester United £1.95
Subscriptions Tel: 0161-877 8852

SOUTH STAND
Seats 9,855
Board Room
Directors Private Room
Disabled Seating
Disabled Toilets
Europa Suite
8 Executive Boxes
Fast Food
First Aid Station
Grill Room
Licensed Bar
Lifts
Police Room
Premier Lounge
Press Rooms
Stretford Suite
Toilets
Trafford Suite
VIP Lounge
Warwick Suite

EAST STAND
Seats 9,802
45 Executive Boxes
Fast Food
First Aid Station
Licensed Bar
Lift
Soft Drinks
Toilets

WEST STAND
Seats 10,398
10 Executive Boxes
Fast Food
First Aid Station
International Suite
Licensed Bar
Lifts
Soft Drinks
Toilets

Disabled Access
South East Lower
37 Wheelchairs,
37 Helpers

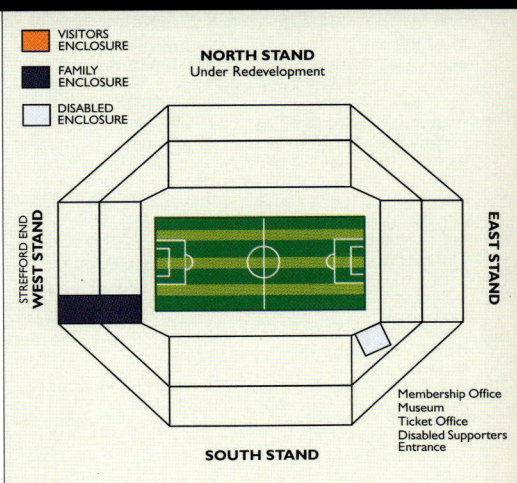

- VISITORS ENCLOSURE
- FAMILY ENCLOSURE
- DISABLED ENCLOSURE

NORTH STAND Under Redevelopment
WEST STAND / STRETFORD END
EAST STAND
SOUTH STAND

Membership Office
Museum
Ticket Office
Disabled Supporters Entrance

MANCHESTER UNITED

GETTING TO THE GAME

Manchester United play at Old Trafford, two miles south-west of Manchester city centre. Parking is available at several paying car parks in the immediate vicinity of the ground, and there are some spaces along Trafford Road. Avoid parking in the nearby residential streets.

BY CAR

From the **North:** From the M6, exit at Junction 21a to join the M62 Eastbound. Exit at Junction 12 onto the M63, and exit the M63 at Junction 7 onto the A56 Chester Road. Continue for 2 miles and turn left into Warwick Road. Old Trafford is on the left.

Or, from the M61, follow signposts to M63 at Junction 1, and continue along until Junction 7. Bear left into Chester Road (A56) to Manchester. Two miles along, turn left into Warwick Road. Old Trafford is on the left.

From the **South:** From the M6, exit at Junction 19, taking the A556 Stockport road to join the A56 at Altrincham. Follow signs to Manchester. Two miles after the motorway flyover, turn left into Warwick Road. Old Trafford is on the left.

From the **East:** From the M62, exit at Junction 17 onto the A56 Bury New Road into Manchester. Follow signs for South, through the City Centre, and then signs for Chester. Two miles past the Bridgewater Viaduct, turn right into Warwick Road. Old Trafford is on the left.

Alternative route for **North, South & West:** From the M62, turn off at the M602 Salford Motorway, and continue to the end. Then turn right at the roundabout into Trafford Road (A5063). Follow for one mile, over the swing bridge, straight over the roundabout, turning right into Chester Road (A56). Warwick Road is the first turning on the right. Old Trafford is on the left.

From the **West:** From the M62, exit at Junction 12 onto the M63. Exit the M63 at Junction 7, turning left into Chester Road (A56). Two miles along, turn left into Warwick Road. Old Trafford is on the left.

BY TRAIN

There is a railway station at the ground (Warwick Road Station), direct from Manchester Oxford Road Station.

The nearest Metrolink station is Old Trafford.

BY BUS

The nearest bus station is Chorley Street.
From Piccadilly Station, nos. 114, 115, 252, 253, 256, 257.
From Victoria Station, no. 264.

IN THE AREA

RADIO

Piccadilly Gold Sport - 103 FM, 1152 AM: Sat 1 - 6pm, pre-match and after-match phone-in, plus live commentaries of top local games. Also Sunday pm if Premier League match on.

GMR - 95.1 FM: 2 - 6pm Sat., reporting live from local big games; also 2.30 - 6pm Sun., 7 - 10pm Tue, Wed., if match on, and hourly sports report.

TOBY RESTAURANTS

Roe Cross Toby Restaurant
Roe Cross Road, Mottram En Longendale, Stockport, Greater Manchester SK14 6FD, tel: 01457-763 147.

Windmill Toby Restaurant
Hulme Road, Denton, Manchester M34 2WZ, tel: 0161-320 6144.

Rudyard
271 Wellington Road, Stockport, Greater Manchester SK4 5BP, tel: 0161-432 2753.

RESTAURANTS

Royal Orchid Thai
From £12 per head, 36 Charlotte Street, M1 4FD, tel: 0161-236 5183.

Brasserie St. Pierre
From £30 per head, 57/63 Princess Street, M2 4EQ, tel: 0161-228 0231.

HOTELS / B&B

Holiday Inn
303 ensuite rooms, restaurants, bars, indoor pool, Crowne Plaza, Peter Street, Manchester M60 2DS, tel: 0161-228 2241, from £96 per double room, incl. breakfast.

The Pinewood Thistle Hotel
58 rooms, Terrace restaurant, free parking, nr. airport, Wilmslow Road, Handford, SK9 3LG, tel: 01625-529 211, rooms from £79.

Blooms Hotel
31 rooms, all mod. cons., restaurant, bar, 11 Bloom Street, M1 3HS, tel: 0161-236 7198, rooms from £35.

Bourneville Hotel
12 rooms, 7 suites, all mod. cons., restaurant, bar, 148 Barlow Moor Road, West Didsbury, M20 2UT, tel: 0161-434 6733, from £15.

Tourist Information Centre: 0161-234 3157

MANCHESTER UNITED FC

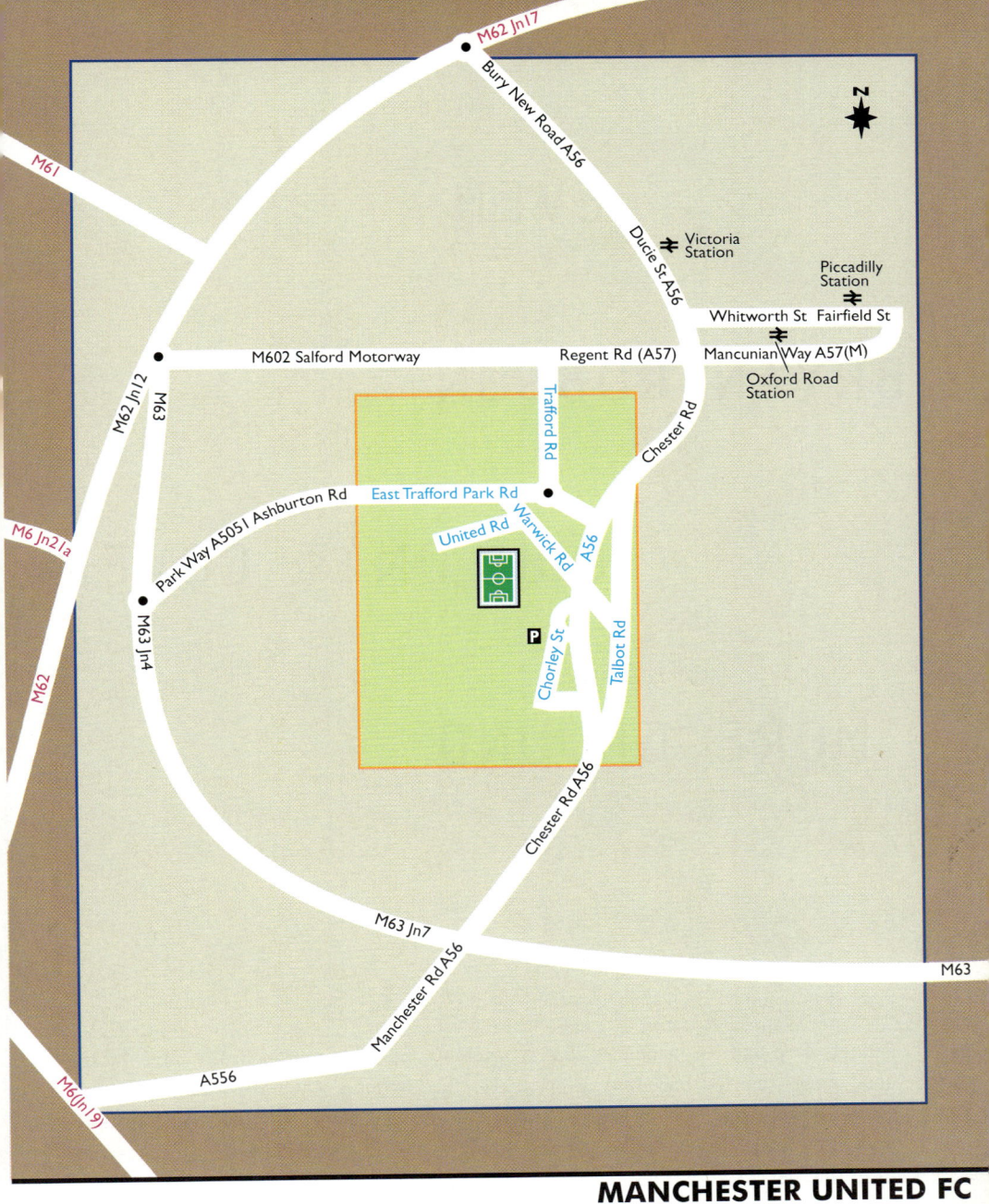

For full match commentary — **PICCADILLY RADIO 1152 AM** — **Always number one for sport**

EVEN

BRYAN ROBSON

COULDN'T COVER

MORE GROUND.

Cellnet is proud to announce its sponsorship of Middlesbrough FC. And that's good news for football fans everywhere. Our national coverage means you can phone home, even when you're away. Call us on 0800 21 4000, or pop into Boro's fantastic new Cellnet Riverside Stadium and find out more about connecting with the net. It's a great result for football, Bryan.

CELLNET AND BORO. A TEAM WORTH SHOUTING ABOUT.

THE NET THAT SETS YOU FREE.   cellnet

MIDDLESBROUGH FC

Club Number: 01642-227 227
Tickets: 01642-227 227
Boro Livewire: 0891-42 42 00
*Calls cost 39p/min. cheap, 49p/min. other times

MFC BORO

Cellnet Riverside Stadium
Middlesbrough
Cleveland
TS3 6RS

Boro Club Shop
Cellnet Riverside Stadium
Mon-Fri: 9.30am - 5pm
Sat. Match Days: 10am - 2.45pm,
plus 45 mins. after the game
Sun. Match Days: 12pm - 3.30pm
Match Eves: 9.30am - 7.30pm
Tel: 01642-227 227

TICKETS

Booking Information

General Enquiries: 01642-227 227
Recorded Information: 0891-42 42 00*
Credit Card Bookings: 01642-227 227
Travel Club: 01642-227 227
Football in the Community: 01642-227 227

Special Packages

Restaurant Facilities: for matchday and non-matchday packages, contact Helen Coverdale: 01642-227 227

Stadium Tours, contact the Public Relations Department: 01642-227 227

Corporate Hospitality & Sponsorship Packages, contact Graham Fordy: 01642-227 227

Match Day Prices Season 1995/96

	Adult	Jun/Sen.Cit.
West Stand		
Upper Tier	£15	n/a
Lower Tier	£12	£6
Family Enclosure	£12	£6
East Stand		
Upper Tier	£14	£10
Lower Tier	£12	£6
Family Enclosure	£12	£6
North Stand	£10	£6
South Stand		
Away Enclosure	£12	£8
Family Enclosure	£8	£4

STADIUM

Programme £1.50

Official Magazine
Red Roar £1.95

Fanzines
Fly Me to the Moon £1

WEST STAND
Seats 8,995
Fast Food
Ladbrokes
Licensed Bar
Merchandise
Programme Booth
Televisions
Toilets

EAST STAND
Seats 7,193
Fast Food
Ladbrokes
Licensed Bar
Merchandise
Programme Booth
Televisions
Toilets

SOUTH STAND
Seats 6,900
Fast Food
Ladbrokes
Licensed Bar
Merchandise
Programme Booth
Televisions
Toilets

NORTH STAND
Seats 7,030
Fast Food
Ladbrokes
Licensed Bar
Merchandise
Programme Booth
Televisions
Toilets

Disabled Access
All Stands,
360 Wheelchairs,
1 Helper per person

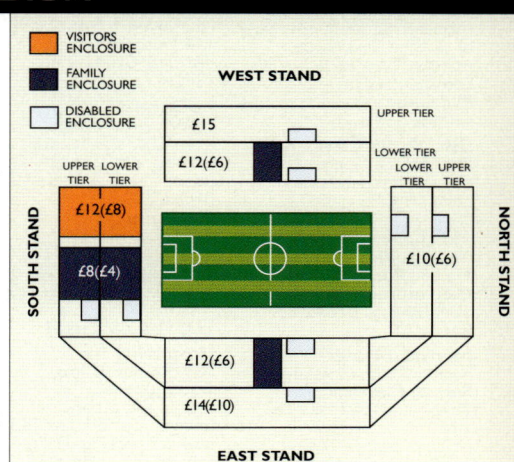

- VISITORS ENCLOSURE
- FAMILY ENCLOSURE
- DISABLED ENCLOSURE

WEST STAND
UPPER TIER £15
LOWER TIER £12(£6)

SOUTH STAND
UPPER TIER £12(£8)
LOWER TIER £8(£4)

NORTH STAND
LOWER TIER £10(£6)
UPPER TIER

EAST STAND
£12(£6)
£14(£10)

MIDDLESBROUGH

GETTING TO THE GAME

Middlesbrough has recently moved into its new stadium - the Cellnet Riverside Stadium. The Cellnet Riverside Stadium is situated in the Middlehaven development area of Middlesbrough, alongside the old Middlesbrough Docks and 15 minutes walk from the town centre. At the time of going to press, access roads were still being constructed and it is not recommended that fans should attempt to park close to the stadium. Also, it should be noted that the Police and Highway Authority had not yet agreed details of car access to the stadium. Parking around the stadium perimeter will be available to pass-holders only. The best bet for car parking is either in the car park on Dock Street, or in one of the car-parks in the town centre.

BY CAR

From the **North:** From the A19, turn left onto the Northern Route (A66) east-bound. Exit the A66 for St. Hilda's and take the first left exit off the roundabout. Follow this road through the traffic lights and into Dock Street. Car Parking is situated on the right. Alternatively, turn right into Albert Road to use town centre car parking and street car parking.

Alternative route from the **North:** From the A19 turn left onto the Northern Route and follow round for 1.3 miles to the junction after the St. Hilda's exit. Come off the A66 onto Marton Road. There are two large car parks, one either side of Marton Road, next to the roundabout. Then take the walkway to the Cellnet Riverside Stadium.

From the **South:** Take the A19 all the way to Middlesbrough, until the junction with the A66, south of the River Tees. Turn right onto the Northern Route (A66), and follow for 2 miles. Then same as from the North.

From the **West:** Approach on the A66, crossing the river on the Tees Bridge, and follow round the Northern Route. Then same as from the North.

BY TRAIN

Middlesbrough Station is situated on Albert Road, and is ten minutes walk away from the stadium: Leave the station and head towards the Hospitality Inn. Cross over the road into the large car park opposite the Odeon, and walk through the car park towards the garage. Enter down into the subway, under the A66, direct to the stadium.

BY BUS

Bus services were still to be confirmed at time of going to press.

IN THE AREA

RADIO

TFM - 96.6 FM: Sat 2pm - 5pm, reviews, build-up, results, round-up, coverage of all Premier League matches plus exclusive live commentary of Middlesbrough F.C.'s games - home and away.

BBC Radio Cleveland - 95.0 FM: Sat 2 pm- 6pm, commentary, interviews, news, results.

TOBY RESTAURANTS

Marton Way Toby Hotel
Marton Road, Middlesbrough, Cleveland TS4 3BS, tel: 01642-817 651.

Mermaid Hotel
Redcar Road, Marske, Redcar, Cleveland TS11 6EX, tel: 01642-483 163.

RESTAURANTS

Pierre Victoire
Continental, a la carte, 3 course lunch from £4.90, 144 Linthorpe Road, TS1 3RA, tel: 01642-220 123.

La Cucard
French & European, from £20, less in early evening, 48 Borough Road, TS1 5DW, tel: 01642-230 531.

Central Park
American, English, European, from £12, 337 Linthorpe Road, TS5 7AA, tel: 01642-820 586

HOTELS / B&B

Hospitality Inn
184 ensuite rooms, water garden, restaurant, bar, 3 bars, lounge, all mod. facilities, free car parking, Fry Streeet, TS1 1JH, tel: 01642-232 000, from £71 per double room.

Highfield Hotel
23 ensuite rooms, bar, restaurant, all mod. cons., free parking, 358 Marton Road, TS4 2PA, tel: 01642-817 638, from £35.95 per double room.

Longlands Hotel
17 rooms, all mod. cons., restaurant, bar, no smoking policy, 295 Martin Road, TS4 2HF, tel: 01642-244 900, from £30 per double room.

PLACES TO VISIT

Nature's World at the Botanic Centre
Innovative environmental centre with organic demonstration gardens, plus much more, Ladgate Lane, Acklam, TS5 7YN, tel: 01642-594 895, Open April-Sept daily 11am - 6pm, Oct-Mar Wed-Sun 11am - 4pm, Adults £1.50, Juniors 50p.

Captain Cook Birthplace Museum
Permanent exhibition charting the life and voyages of Captain James Cook, cafe, gift shop, Stewart Park, Marton, TS7 6AS, tel: 01642-311 211, Open Winter, Adults £1.30, Juniors 65p, Family £3.20.

Cleveland Crafts Centre
Thriving museum and gallery, shop, 57 Gilkes Street, TS1 5EL, tel: 01642-226 351, Open Tues-Sat 10am - 5pm, admission free.

Tourist Information Centre: 01642-243 425

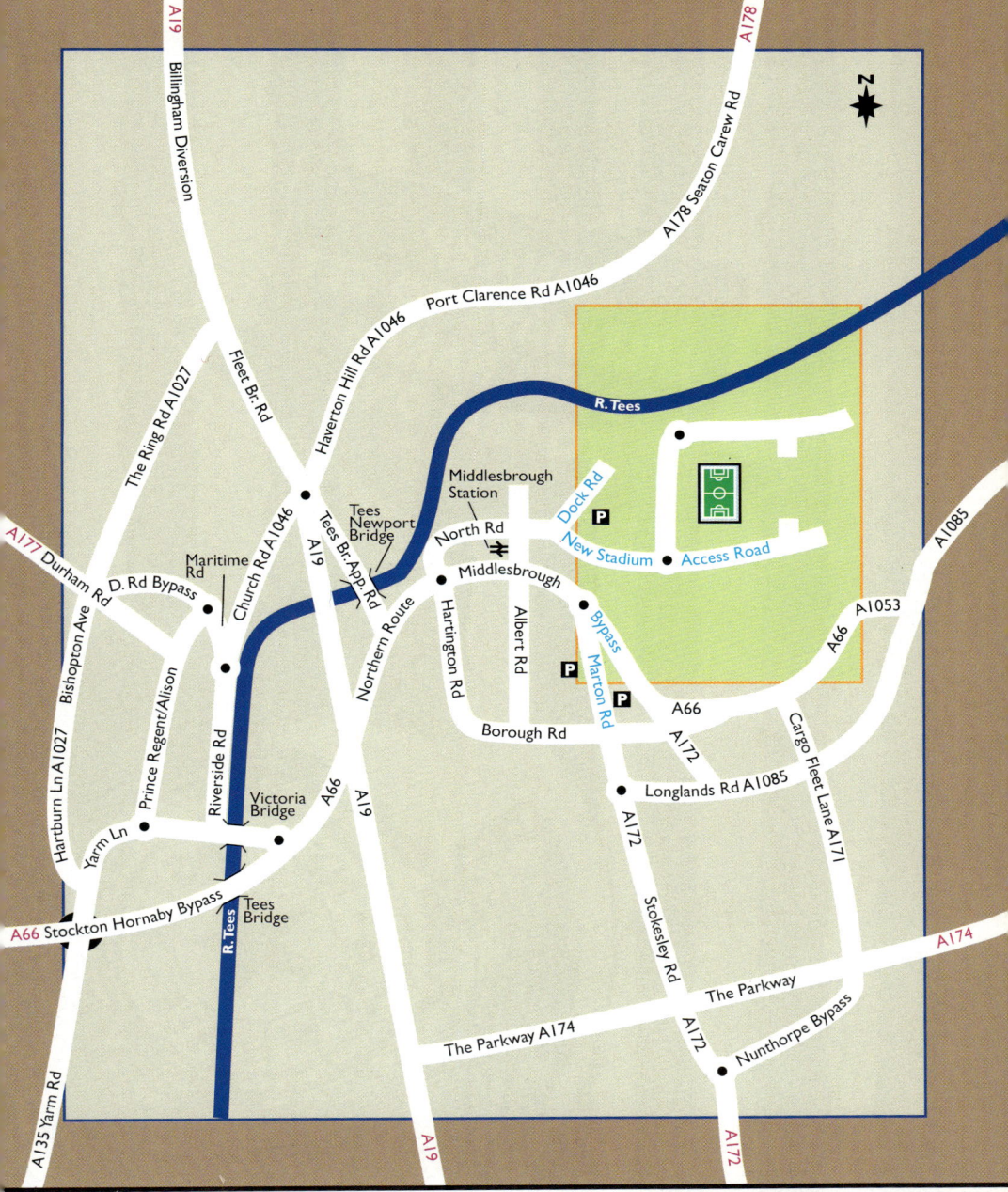

MIDDLESBROUGH FC

The Sports Leader
Saturdays 2 - 5pm

FM 96·6

SRNICEK WILL HAVE TO GET BOTH HANDS TO THIS ONE.

NEWCASTLE BROWN ALE

Britain's biggest bottled beer

NEWCASTLE UNITED FC

Club Number: 0191-232 8361
Tickets: 0191-261 1571
Club Call: 0891-12 11 90
*Calls cost 39p/min. cheap, 49p/min. other times

NUFC MAGPIES

St. James' Park
Newcastle-Upon-Tyne
NE1 4ST

Newcastle United Official Store
St. James' Park Stadium
Mon-Fri: 9am - 5pm
Sat Match Days: 9am - 6pm
Sun Match Days: 10am - 6pm
Match Eves: 9am - 10pm
Tel: 0191-261 6357
Mail Order: 0191-232 4080

Newcastle United Official Store
Eldon Square, Newcastle-Upon-Tyne
Mon-Fri: 9am - 5.30pm, Thurs: 9am - 8pm
Sat Match Days: 9am - 6pm
Tel: 0191-230 0808

TICKETS

Booking Information

General Enquiries: 0191-261 1571
Credit Card Bookings: 0191-261 1571
Travel Club: 0191-221 1000

Special Packages

Stadium Tours, contact Claire Savage: 0191-232 8361

Corporate Hospitality & Sponsorship Packages, contact Trevor Garwood or Carol Raphael: 0191-232 3050

Match Day Prices Season 1995/96

East Stand
Main Block
Paddock
Family Enclosure

Milburn Stand
Main Block
Paddock

Sir John Hall Stand

Exhibition Stand

NOT DECIDED AT TIME OF GOING TO PRESS.

STADIUM

Programme £1.50

Official Magazine
Black and White
£2.50

Fanzines
The Mag
£1
The Number Nine
£0p
Talk of the Toon
£1
Half Mag Half Biscuit
£1
The Giant Awakes
£1
Talk of the Tyne
£1
Toon Army News
£1

EAST STAND
Seats 4,941
Executive Boxes
Fast Food Kiosks
(alcohol sold)
Ladbrokes
Toilets

MILBURN STAND
Seats 8,713
Directors Box
Executive Boxes
Fast Food Kiosks
Ladbrokes
Licensed Bar
Toilets

SIR JOHN HALL STAND
Seats 11,037
Fast Food Kiosks
Ladbrokes
Licensed Bar

Players' Box
Toilets

EXHIBITION STAND
Seats 11,872
Executive Boxes
Fast Food Kiosks
Ladbrokes
Licensed Bar
Restaurant
Toilets

Disabled Access
Sir John Hall Stand
74 Wheelchairs, 1 Helper per person;
Exhibition Stand
20 Wheelchairs, 1 Helper per person

VISITORS ENCLOSURE
FAMILY ENCLOSURE
DISABLED ENCLOSURE

ST. JAMES' STREET
EAST STAND

SIR JOHN HALL STAND

STRAWBERRY PLACE
EXHIBITION STAND

MILBURN STAND
BARRACK ROAD

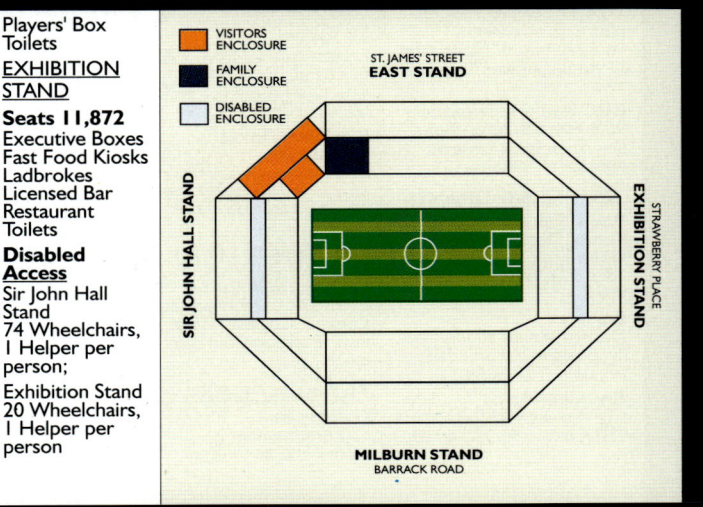

Getting to the Game

Newcastle United play at St. James' Park, half a mile from Newcastle city centre. The Newcastle metro system is very efficient, and there is a station by the ground. Car parking is frequently directed by police as you approach the ground, and there is a car park along Barrack Road, as well as one just north of the stadium.

By Car

From the **North:** Travel along the A1 until the junction with the A69 and A186. Take the left exit at the roundabout into West Road (A168) to Newcastle. Continue for 2½ miles and turn left into Corporation Street. At the end roundabout, Barrack Road is to the left, and Gallowgate to the right. Police will be there to issue directions to appropriate car parking.

Alternative route from the **North:** Use A1 into Newcastle, exiting left at the junction with the A696 and A167 into Ponteland Road (A167). At the fourth roundabout continue left along Jedburgh Road (A167). At the next interchange, exit left to go right over Jedburgh Road. Continue along Grandstand Road for 200 metres. Flow left into Ponteland Road, and continue over the next junction with the BBC building to the left. Approx. 50 metres past the junction turn left for car parking. The ground is 400 metres further down Barrack Road.

From the **South:** Take the A1 until the interchange with the A184. Go into Derwentwater Road (A184), cross the Tyne on the New Redheugh Bridge and continue into Blenheim Street. Cross over Westgate into Rutherford Street. Turn left into Bath Lane and first right into Corporation Street. At the end roundabout, Barrack Road is to the left and Gallowgate to the right. Police will be there to issue directions to appropriate car parking.

Alternative route from the **South:** Take the A1 until junction with the A186 and A69. Turn right at roundabout into West Road (A186). Then same as from the North.

From the **West:** Take A69 to junction with the A1 and A186. Go straight over roundabout into West Road (A186). Then same as from the North.

By Train

Newcastle Central Railway Station (tel: 0191-232 6262) is half a mile from St James' Park. Downstairs you can catch the metro - every 3-4 mins - to St. James' Station (Metro Service tel: 0191-232 5325).

In The Area

Radio

Metro Radio - 97.1 FM & 103 FM:: Sat 2pm - 5pm, reviews, build-up, results, round-up, coverage of all Premier League matches plus exclusive live commentary of Newcastle United's games - home and away.

BBC Radio Newcastle - 95.4 FM: Sat 2pm - 6pm, live coverage, previews, interviews, results.

Toby Restaurants

Bank Top Toby Hotel Kenton Bank, Newcastle-Upon-Tyne, Tyne and Wear NE3 3TY, tel: 0191-214 0877.

Barnes Durham Road, Sunderland, Tyne and Wear SR2 7RB, tel: 0191-528 5644.

Branding Arms High Street, Gosforth, NE3 1HD, tel: 0191-285 6718

Restaurants

Comedy Cafe Tosca's Bistro, Tyne Theatre, Westgate Rd, NE1 7RH, tel: 0191-232 0899

Le Rivage French cuisine, from £20 per head, The Close, The Quayside, NE1 3RT, tel: 0191-222 0333.

Big Lukes Texas Restaurant American tucker, from £6 a head, 45 Bath Lane, NE4 5SP, tel: 0191-230 1022.

Eldon Square Leisure Centre City Centre, NE1, tel: 0191-221 0119 Mexican, Burgers, Chinese, Pizza, Fish, Traditional Sunday lunch.

Hotels / B&B

Holiday Inn 150 ensuite rooms, restaurant, bar, indoor pool, games room, free parking, Great North Road, Seaton Burn, Newcastle-Upon-Tyne NE13 6BP, tel: 0191-236 5432, from £72 per double room, incl. breakfast.

The County Thistle Hotel 115 rooms, free overnight parking, restaurant, bar, 7 meeting rooms, Neville St, NE99 1AH, tel: 0191-232 2471, Prices from £40 per person incl. breakfast.

The Wheatsheaf 10 rooms, restaurant, bar, children's play areas, Callerton Lane Ends, Woolsington, NE13 8DF, tel: 0191-286 9254, Rooms from £39.95 per person per night, incl. breakfast.

Places to Visit

Sea Life Centre A Journey under the sea - without getting wet, Grand Parade, Tynemouth, NE3 4JF, tel: 0191-257 6100, Open 7 days 10am - 5pm, Adults £3.95, Juniors £2.95, Under 4's free.

Tynemouth Priory and Castle Famous dramatic clifftop landmark, East Street, North Shields, NE30 4BZ, tel: 0191-257 1090, Open April - Sept: Daily 10am - 8pm; Oct - Mar: Tues-Sun 10am - 6pm, Adults £1.20, Conc. 60p-90p.

Metrocentre Europe's biggest shopping and leisure centre, 360 shops, 11 cinemas, 3 miles from the city centre, late night shopping, theme shopping.

Tourist Information Centre: 0191-261-6262

NEWCASTLE UNITED FC

Tune Army
Saturdays 2 - 5.15pm

Metro fm 97.1

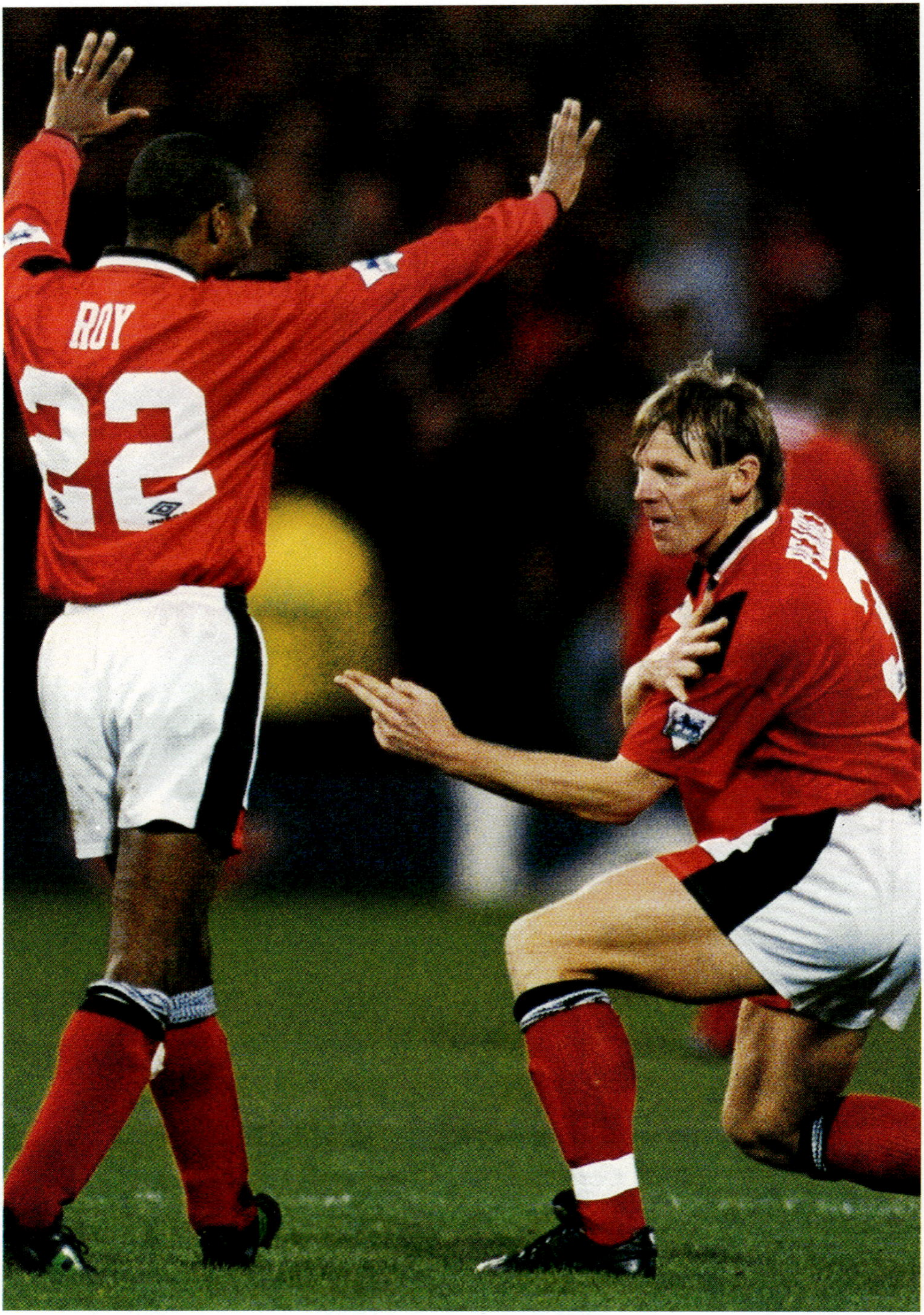
ROY
22

NOTTINGHAM FOREST FC

Club Number: 0115-952 6000
Tickets: 0115-952 6002
Club Call: 0891-12 11 74
*Calls cost 39p/min. cheap, 49p/min. other times

NFFC FOREST

City Ground
Nottingham
NG2 5FJ

Souvenir Shop
City Ground Stadium
Mon-Fri: 9am - 5pm
Sat. Match Days: 9am - 3pm,
plus 30 mins after the game
Sun. Match Days: 9am - kickoff,
plus 30 mins after the game
Match Eves: 9am - kickoff,
plus 30 mins after the game
Tel: 0115-952 6026
Fax: 0115-952 6007

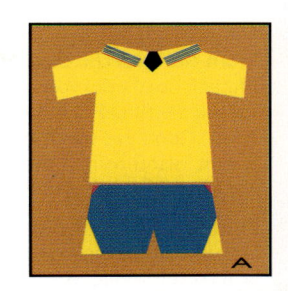

TICKETS

Booking Information
General Enquiries: 0115-952 6002
Recorded Information: 0115-952 6016
Credit Card Bookings: 0115-952 6024
Junior Reds: 0115-952 6001
Forest in the Community,
contact Gordon Coleman: 0115-952 6006

Special Packages
Restaurant Facilities: 0115-952 6015
Museum opening 1995/96 in Trent End concourse
Stadium Tours, 2 hour tour,
Adults £4.95, Children £2.95: 0115-952 6006
Corporate Hospitality & Sponsorship Packages,
contact the Commercial Office: 0115-952 6006

Match Day Prices Season 1995/96

Bridgford Stand	
Upper Tier	£17
Lower Tier (Visitors)	£16
Main Stand	£18
Trent End	
Upper Tier	£17
Lower Tier (Family) Adult	£16
Lower Tier (Family) Junior	£8
Executive Stand	
Upper Tier	£17
Lower Tier	£16

Adults only with children under 15 in Family Section.

STADIUM

Programme £1.50

Official Magazine £1.95

Fanzines
The Almighty Brian 70p
Garibaldi £1.00
Forest Forever 50p
The Tricky Tree 50p

BRIDGFORD STAND
Seats 7,710
Fast Food
Ladbrokes
Licensed Bar
Souvenir Shop
Toilets

MAIN STAND
Seats 5,708
Fast Food
Licensed Bar
Snack Bar
Toilets

TRENT END
Seats 6,770
Fast Food
Ladbrokes (Upper Tier)
Licensed Bar
Snack Bar
Souvenir Shop
Toilets

EXECUTIVE STAND
Seats 9,788;
Boxes 288
Fast Food
Ladbrokes
Licensed Bar (Lower Tier)
Snack bar
Souvenir Shop
Toilets

Disabled Access
Bridgford Upper, 15 Wheelchairs, 28 Helpers;
Bridgford Lower, 22 Wheelchairs, 22 Helpers;
Trent End Lower, 22 Wheelchairs, 22 Helpers.

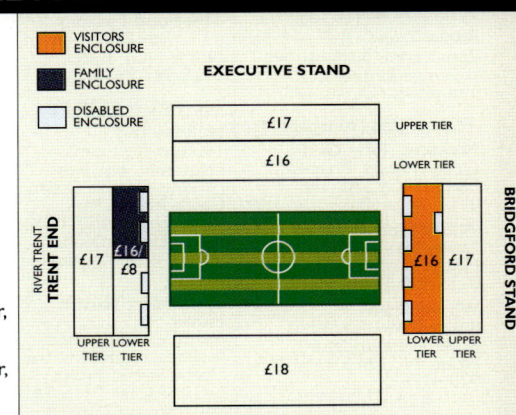

NOTTINGHAM FOREST

GETTING TO THE GAME

Nottingham Forest play at the City Ground situated south of Nottingham city centre and the River Trent, opposite Trent Bridge Cricket Ground. The visitors are accommodated in the Lower Tier of the Bridgford Stand. Access to the visitors' turnstiles is through the East Stand car park via Scarrington Road off Lady Bay Bridge. Parking prohibitions are in force on match days around the ground. Nottingham Council operates a paying car park 15-20 minutes walk away on Victoria Embankment. Access is via Clifton Bridge complex to Queens Drive and then Riverside Way. South of the river, in West Bridgford it is permitted to park in the side streets.

BY CAR

From the **North**: Leave the M1 at Junction 26, following the signs to Nottingham via the A610 Nuthall Road until you meet the Nottingham Ring Road A6514 at Western Boulevard. Turn right and follow the Ring Road south, passing the Queens Medical Centre where the Ring Road becomes the A52. Continue south on the A52 signposted Grantham over Clifton Bridge, past the Nottingham Knight Island to join the Lings Bar Road at the next traffic island. Continue to the Gamston Island and then turn left into Radcliffe Road (A6011). Turn right into Colwick Road.

From the **South**: Leave the M1 at Junction 24, on the A453, towards Nottingham. At the Clifton Bridge complex follow signs A52 Grantham past Nottingham Knight Island to join the Lings Bar Road at the next traffic island. Follow the A52 signposted Grantham to the Gamston Island and then turn left into Radcliffe Road (A6011). Turn right into Colwick Road.

From the **East**: Approach via the A52 Radcliffe Road from Grantham. At Gamston Island continue along Radcliffe Road as it becomes the A6011. Turn right into Colwick Road.

From the **West**: Approach via the A52 from Derby to the Nottingham Ring Road, along the Stapleford Bypass. Turn right onto the Ring Road (A52) and follow routes as above. Alternatively, from the M42, follow the A453 to the Clifton Bridge complex and follow route as from the South.

BY TRAIN

Nottingham Midland Railway Station (tel: 01332-257 000) is situated in the town centre, approx ½ mile from the ground.

BY BUS

The most convenient bus station is on Collin Street, by the Broadmarsh Shopping Centre. From there, you can take buses 12 or 90, get off just after crossing the river, 2 minutes walk to the ground.

IN THE AREA

RADIO
BBC Radio Nottingham - 103.8 FM, 95.5 FM: Sat 2pm - 6pm, pre-match build-up, live match coverage, results, reviews.

Radio Trent - 999 AM: Sat 2pm - 6pm, build-up, live coverage, previews, interviews.

TOBY RESTAURANTS
Meadow Toby Grill
Queens Road, Chilwell, Notts. NG9 5AE, tel: 0115-943 6184.

Priory Hotel
Derby Road, Wollaton Vale, Notts. NG8 2NR, tel: 0115-922 1691.

Willow Tree
Rufford Way, Stamford Road, West Bridgford, Notts. NG2 6LS, tel: 0115-923 4976.

RESTAURANTS
The Chateau
Wilford Lane, Notts. NG2 7RL, tel: 0115-981 9192

The Food Factory
34 Lower Parliament St, Notts. NG1 3DA, tel: 0115-947 2940

HOTELS / B&B
Holiday Inn
100 ensuite rooms, restaurant, bar, free parking, Garden Court, Castle Marina Park, Nottingham NG7 1GX, tel: 0115-950 0600, from £49.50 per double room.

Strathdon Thistle Hotel
En-suite rooms, mod. facilities, restaurant, bar, Derby Street, Notts. NG1 5FT, tel: 0115-941 8501, from £25 per person per night (incl. breakfast).

Forte Crest Hotel
130 rooms, mod. facilities, restaurant, bar, live music, St James Street, Notts. NG1 6BN, tel: 0115-947 0131, from £29.50 per person per night.

Rutland Square Hotel
Adjacent to the castle, 103 en-suite rooms, mod. facilities, restaurant, St James Street, Notts. NG1 6FJ, tel: 0115-941 1114, from £25 per person per night.

PLACES TO VISIT
Caves of Nottingham
Discover a secret world beneath the streets of Nottingham, Broadmarsh Shopping Centre, NG1 7LF, tel: 0115-924 1424, Mon-Sat, 10am - 5pm Adults £2.75, Juniors £1.50.

The Tales of Robin Hood
Take an adventure ride back in time with sight, sound & smell, 30-38 Maid Marion Way, NG1 6GF, tel: 0115-948 3284 Open 7 days, 10am - 6pm (last entry 4.30pm), Adults £4.25, Juniors £3.25.

AMF Ten Pin Bowling
Bellward Street, NG1 1JZ, tel: 0115-950 5588, Open 7 days, 10am – midnight, £1.60 - £3.30.

Nottingham Ice Rink
The rink Torvill & Dean made famous, Lower Parliament Street, NG1 1LA, tel: 0115-950 1938, Phone for session times, £1.85 - £2.55, plus skate hire.

Tourist Information Centre: 0115-977 3558

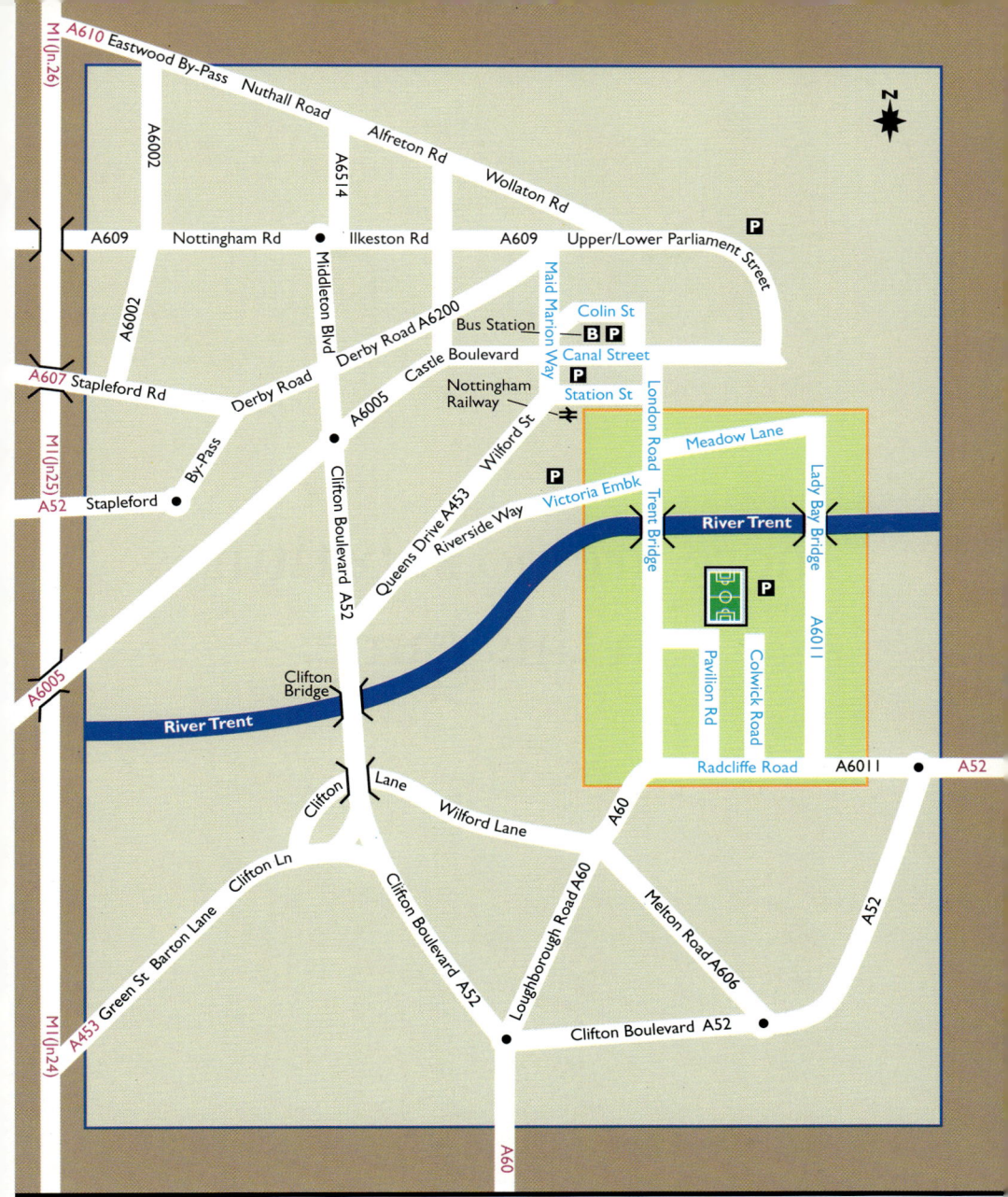

NOTTINGHAM FOREST FC

Radio **NOTTINGHAM 103.8 & 95.5**

"Follow Forest Home and Away with Martin Fisher and Colin Fray."

There are no substitutes
in this game.

COMPAQ

Compaq, the world's No.1 PC manufacturer, are proud to sponsor QPR.

QUEENS PARK RANGERS FC

Club Number: 0181-743 0262
Tickets: 0181-749 5744
Club Call: 0891-12 11 62
*Calls cost 39p/min. cheap, 49p/min. other times

QPRFC RANGERS

Rangers Stadium
South Africa Road
London
W12 7PA

Rangers Clubhouse
Mon-Fri: 9am - 5pm
Sats: 9am - 1pm
Sat. Match Days: 9am - 2.45pm,
plus 30 mins. after the game
Sun. Match Days: 1pm - 3.45pm,
plus 30 mins. after the game
Match Eves: 9am - 7.30pm,
plus 30 mins. after the game
Tel: 0181-749 6862
Fax: 0181-749 8585
Mail Order Service:
Tel: 0181-749 6862

TICKETS

Booking Information
General Enquiries: 0181-749 5744
Recorded Information: 0181-749 7798
Credit Card Bookings: 0171-344 9494
Travel Club: 0181-749 6771

Special Packages
Restaurant Facilities available in the Tony Ingham Suite, contact Lynn Johnson: 0181-740 8737

Stadium Tours, contact Patricia Dix: 0181-749 6771

Corporate Hospitality & Sponsorship Packages, contact Lynn Johnson: 0181-740 8737

Match Day Prices Season 1995/96

	Cat. A	Cat. B
South Africa Road Stand	£20	£15
Ellerslie Road Stand	£16	£13
Juvenile Section (Ellerslie Rd Stand)	£16 (£6)	£13 (£6)
Loftus Road Stand		
Upper Level (Members only)	£10 (£5)	£10 (£5)
Lower Level Members	£10 (£5)	£10 (£5)
Lower Level Non-Members	£12 (£6)	£12 (£6)
East & West Paddocks		
Members	£8 (£4)	£8 (£4)
Non-Members	£10 (£5)	£10 (£5)

Prices in brackets denote Juvenile & Senior Citizen concessions

STADIUM

Programme £1.50

Official Magazine
Rangers Newspaper (Quarterly) £1

Fanzines
In the Loft £1
A Kick up the Rs £1
Beat about the Bush £1
All Quiet on the Western Avenue £1

SOUTH AFRICA ROAD STAND
Seats 5,295
Fast Food
Ladbrokes
Licensed Bar
Toilets

ELLERSLIE ROAD STAND
Seats 4,844
First Aid Station
Fast Food
Ladbrokes
Licensed Bar
Toilets

LOFTUS ROAD STAND
Seats 4,991
Fast Food
Ladbrokes
Licensed Bar
Toilets

SCHOOL END
Seats 3,789
Fast Food
Ladbrokes
Toilets

Disabled Access
Ellerslie Road Stand, 13 Wheelchairs, 20 Helpers

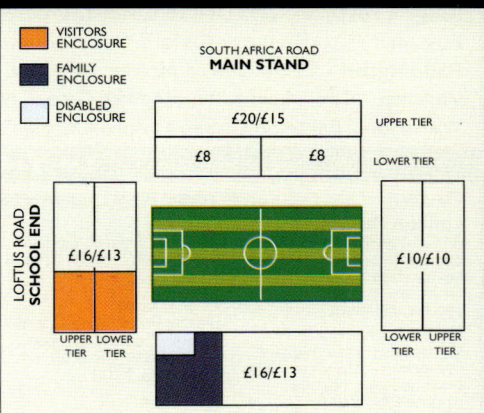

VISITORS ENCLOSURE
FAMILY ENCLOSURE
DISABLED ENCLOSURE

SOUTH AFRICA ROAD MAIN STAND
£20/£15 UPPER TIER
£8 £8 LOWER TIER

LOFTUS ROAD SCHOOL END
£16/£13 UPPER TIER / LOWER TIER

LOFTUS ROAD STAND
£10/£10 LOWER TIER / UPPER TIER

£16/£13
ELLERSLIE ROAD STAND

Getting to the Game

Queens Park Rangers play at Loftus Road in West London, three miles from the city centre. The best bet for parking, if you want to leave your car near the ground, is to turn into Old Oak Road, which runs between Western Avenue and Uxbridge Road and look for space at the Flowers Estate. Take care locking up your car.

By Car

From the **North**: From the M1, follow onto the North Circular Road (A406) westbound. After 4 miles, cross over the Hanger Lane roundabout to the third exit, keeping to the A406. 1¼ miles on, at the next major junction turn left into Uxbridge Road (A4020), and continue along for 2¼ miles. Turn left into Bloemfontein Road, then third right right into South Africa Road. QPR is on the right.

Alternative route: From the M1, follow onto the North Circular Road (A406) westbound. After 2½ miles, turn left into Hillside (A404), signposted Harlseden. Stay on the A404 for 1½ miles, then turn right into Scrubs Lane (A219). Continue under the flyover (A40), and take the first right into South Africa Road. QPR is on the right.

From the **South**: Take the A3 to the A219 Tibbets Ride. Cross the Thames over Putney Bridge, following signs to Hammersmith. Go round the Hammersmith gyratory to rejoin Shepherds Bush Road (A219). Just past Shepherds Bush Green, turn left onto Uxbridge Road (A4020), then fifth turning on the right into Loftus Road. QPR is on the left.

From the **East outside London**: Follow the M11 to the end of the motorway, turning right onto the North Circular Road (A406). Stay on the North Circular for about 15 miles, crossing over the Hanger Lane roundabout. At the next major junction, turn left into Uxbridge Road (A4020), and continue along for 2¼ miles. Turn left into Bloemfontein Road, then third right right into South Africa Road. QPR is on the right.

From the **East inside London**: Join Marylebone Road (A501) to the Westway (A40(M)), and turn left onto the West Cross Route (M41). At the roundabout, take the third exit, and follow the right fork into Uxbridge Road (A4020). Shepherds Bush Green is on your left. Fifth left turn into Loftus Road. QPR is on the left.

From the **West**: Follow the M4 to Chiswick Roundabout, then turn onto Chiswick High Road (A315) for 2½ miles to Hammersmith. Turn left onto Shepherds Bush Road (A219). Just past Shepherds Bush Green, turn left onto Uxbridge Road (A4020), then fifth turning on the right into Loftus Road. QPR is on the left.

By Train

The nearest Underground Stations are White City and Shepherds Bush, both on the Central Line. Shepherds Bush is also on the Hammersmith & City Line.

Kings Cross - Victoria Line to Oxford Circus, Central Line to White City
Euston - Victoria Line to Oxford Circus, Central Line to White City
Paddington - Circle Line to Notting Hill Gate, Central Line to White City
Victoria - Circle Line to Notting Hill Gate, Central Line to White City
Waterloo - Bakerloo Line to Oxford Circus, Central Line to White City

In The Area

Radio

London Radio - 97.3 FM & 1152 AM: 24-hour extensive sports coverage seven days a week, twice an hour - previews, results, reviews.

Radio 5 Live - 909 MW General sports coverage - live commentary on main matches plus regular updated bulletins.

Toby Restaurants

George
213 The Strand, London WC2R 0AP, tel: 0171-353 9238.

White Lion
Derby Road, 24 St. James Street, Covent Garden, London WC2E 8NS, tel: 0171-836 2308.

Red Lion
20 Great Windmill Street, Soho, London W1V 7PH, tel: 0171-437 4635.

Restaurants

Ritz Restaurant
From £20 per head, 33 Goldhawk Road, W12 8QQ, tel: 0181-743 6722

Esarn Kheaw
Thai cuisine, from £20 per head, 314 Uxbridge Road, W12 7LJ, tel: 0181-743 8930

Reds Chicken & Ribs
From £3, 132 Uxbridge Road, W12 8AA, tel: 0181-749 9103

Hotels / B&B

Holiday Inn
162 ensuite rooms, restaurants, bars, leisure facilities, private garden, 100 Cromwell Road, London SW7 4ER, tel: 0171-373 2222, from £165 per double room.

Taxis

Yellow Bird Cars
167a Percy Road, W12 9QJ, tel: 0181-723 5566

QUEENS PARK RANGERS FC

The only sports channel you'll ever need — London news 97.3 fm

WINNING COMPUTER SOLUTIONS

Sanderson Electronics PLC is a leading supplier of premier computer solutions, is listed on the London Stock Exchange and employs more than 700 people in 25 office locations throughout the United Kingdom, Australia, New Zealand and East Asia. Sanderson has an extensive portfolio of application software packages which operate on a wide variety of hardware platforms under open system environments such as UNIX and DOS. Sanderson is committed to providing its 4000 customers with reliable products of a high quality and with a high standard of service and support.

1. Manufacturing
2. Solicitors
3. Credit Management
4. Finance and Distribution
5. Supply Chain Management
6. Police
7. Direct Marketing
8. Local Government
9. Airports
10. Insurance
11. Printing Industry
12. Healthcare
13. Computer Based Training
14. Schools and Colleges
15. Hotels
16. Production Monitoring
17. Processing Industry
18. Media and Publishing

SANDERSO

For Premier Computer Solutions

To obtain further information please tick the relevant box(es) and return a copy of this advertisement with your business card to :-
Sanderson Electronics PLC, Parkway House, Parkway Avenue, Sheffield S9 4WA, or alternatively Telephone (0114) 2827777 or Fax (0114) 2821340

Name _____

Position _____

Address _____

_____

_____

Tel. No. _____

SHEFFIELD WEDNESDAY FC

Club Number: 0114-234 3122
Tickets: 0114-233 7233
Club Call: 0891-12 11 86
*Calls cost 39p/min. cheap, 49p/min. other times

SWFC OWLS

Hillsborough
Sheffield
S6 1SW

S.W.F.C. Superstore
Hillsborough Stadium
Mon-Fri: 9am - 5pm, Thur: 9am - 7pm
Sat Match Days: 9am - 3pm
Sun Match Days: 9am - 4pm
Match Eves: 9am - 7.45pm
Non-match Sats: 9am - 4pm
Tel: 0114-234 3342

Wednesday Gear
Orchard Square Shopping Centre, Sheffield
Mon-Sat: 9am - 5.30pm
Tel: 0114-275 1443

TICKETS

Booking Information
General Enquiries: 0114-233 7233
Recorded Information: 0114-234 3122
Credit Card Bookings: 0114-234 3122
Travel Club: 0114-234 9906

Special Packages
Restaurant Facilities,
contact Commercial Department: 0114-233 7235
Stadium Tours,
contact Charlie Williamson: 0114-231 3684
Corporate Hospitality & Sponsorship Packages,
contact Sean O'Toole: 0114-233 7235

Match Day Prices Season 1995/96

	Premier	Standard
North Stand	£17 (£11.50)	£12.50 (£8.50)
West Stand		
Upper Tier	£12.50 (£8.50)	£12.50 (£8.50)
Lower Tier	£11.50 (£6.50)	£8.50 (£5)
South Stand	£17 (£11.50)	£12.50 (£8.50)
Spion Kop	£11.50 (£6.50)	£8.50 (£5)
North West Terrace	£11.50 (£6.50)	£8.50 (£5)

Prices in brackets denote concessions.

STADIUM

Programme
£1.50

Fanzines
A View from the East Bank
£1
The Blue & White Lizard
£1
Boddle
80p
War of the Monster Trucks
50p
Cheat
30p

NORTH STAND
Seats 9,000
3 Snack Bars
SWFC Superstore
Toilets
Disabled Toilets

WEST STAND
Seats 6,500
2 Snack Bars
Toilets

SOUTH STAND
Seats 8,000
Under extensive re-development, for banqueting suites, function rooms and full entertainment facilities

SPION KOP
Seats 11,000
3 Snack Bars
Toilets

NORTH WEST TERRACE
Seats 1,300
Snack Bar
Toilets

Disabled Access
North Stand & West Stand Lower Tier
80 Wheelchairs, 100 Ambulant disabled, 80 Helpers.

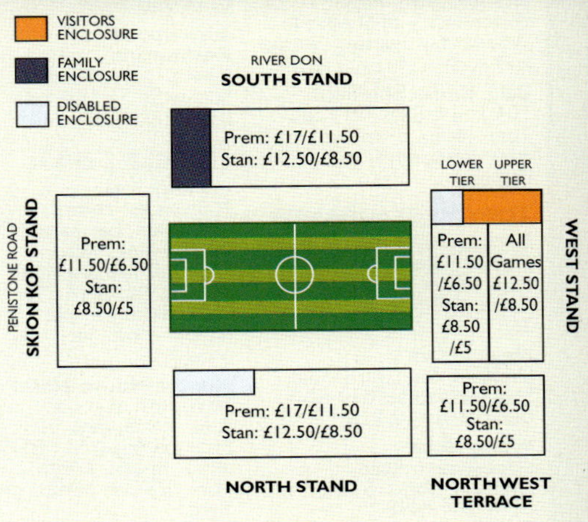

- VISITORS ENCLOSURE
- FAMILY ENCLOSURE
- DISABLED ENCLOSURE

RIVER DON
SOUTH STAND
Prem: £17/£11.50
Stan: £12.50/£8.50

PENISTONE ROAD
SKION KOP STAND
Prem: £11.50/£6.50
Stan: £8.50/£5

WEST STAND
LOWER TIER / UPPER TIER
Prem: £11.50/£6.50
Stan: £8.50
All Games £12.50/£8.50

NORTH STAND
Prem: £17/£11.50
Stan: £12.50/£8.50

NORTH WEST TERRACE
Prem: £11.50/£6.50
Stan: £8.50/£5

GETTING TO THE GAME

Sheffield Wednesday's Stadium is situated 2 miles from the city centre. At present major road works are taking place throughout Sheffield as construction of the 'Supertram' system gets underway. For the current season, all visitors are recommended to approach via the M1/A61 route, and to avoid the city centre. Please allow sufficient time for travelling in the event of further disruption to the road network. Parking is possible in the area just north of Hillsborough around Doe Royd Lane and Lyminster Road.

BY CAR

From the **North, South, East & West:** From the M1 - (if approaching via the M57, join the M1 at Junction 31) - exit at Junction 36 onto the A61 into Sheffield. Continue along Penistone Road (A61) for approx. eight miles. Hillsborough Stadium is on the right.

Alternative route from the **North:** Leave the M1 at Junction 34, taking the Sheffield Town exit - the A6109 Meadow Hall Road. After 1¼ miles, turn right into Upwell Street (A6102). Cross over Barnsley Road (A6135) into Herries Road. Stay on this road for about 2½ miles until the T-junction at Penistone Road (A61). Hillsborough Stadium is opposite.

Alternative route from the **South & East:** Leave the M1 at Junction 34, taking the second left turn at the roundabout into Common Sheffield Road (A6178). After about 1 mile turn right into Janson Street (A6102) which becomes Hawke Street. Cross over East Brightside Lane (A6109) and into Upwell Street. Follow this road, crossing over Barsley Road (A6135) into Herries Road. Stay on this road for about 2½ miles until the T-junction at Penistone Road (A61). Hillsborough Stadium is opposite.

Alternative route from the **West:** Take the A57 for Sheffield, and take the left fork for Rivelin Valley Road (A6101). After 3 miles, turn right into Holme Lane which becomes Bradfield Road. At the junction with Penistone Road, turn left. Half a mile on, Hillsborough Stadium is on the left.

BY TRAIN

Sheffield Railway Station (tel: 01254 662537) is situated in the town centre, approx. 2 miles from the ground.

BY BUS

From the Railway Station, Flat Street Bus Terminus is a one-minute walk: cross over at the pedestrian crossing, and follow signs. Head for the far side of the terminus. Bus no. 53 to Ecclesfield runs regularly to the ground from Flat Street.

IN THE AREA

RADIO

Hallam FM - 97.4 FM & 103.4 FM - coverage of all Premier League matches plus exclusive live commentary of Sheffield Wednesday's games - home and away.

BBC Radio Sheffield - 104.1 FM, 88.6 FM - Sat 2pm - 6pm, previews, interviews, coverage, results.

TOBY RESTAURANTS

Crosspool Tavern Toby Carving Room
Manchester Road, Sheffield, Yorks. S10 5DT, tel: 0114-266 2113.

Nags Head
Sheffield Road, Dronfield, Sheffield, Yorks. S18 6GA, tel: 01246-412 326.

White Rose
Handsworth Road, Sheffield, Yorks. S9 9BY, tel: 0114-244 4498.

RESTAURANTS

Channings
from £20 per head, 617 London Rd, S2 4HT, tel: 0114-250 7577.

Tuckwoods Restaurant
from £12 per head, Surrey St, S1 1DP, tel: 0114-272 1080.

HOTELS / B&B

Holiday Inn
100 ensuite rooms, restaurant, bar, satellite, free parking, Victoria Station Road, Sheffield S4 7YE, tel: 0114-276 8822, from £54 per double room, incl. breakfast.

Hunter House Hotel
10 rooms, all mod. cons., restaurant, 685 Ecclesall Road, S11 8TG, tel: 0114-266 2709, from £25 per person per night.

Ivory House Hotel
34 Wostenholm Road, Nether Edge, S7 1LJ, tel: 0114-255 1853, from £18 per person per night.

PLACES TO VISIT

Quasar
Laser gun team game, available individually or in groups, Halifax Road, Wadsley Bridge, S6 1NN, tel: 0114-233 0011, Open 7 days, 10am - 10.45pm, £2.75 eves/ w'ends, £1.75 at other times.

South Yorkshire Railway
Over 25 engines and all the gear, with plans for a 3½ mile line from Meadowbank to Chapeltown. Experience real steam locomotion. Barrow Road, Meadowbank, tel: 0114-242 4405 (John Wade), Open 7 days, 11am - 4 pm, Adults £2, Conc. less.

Hillsborough Leisure Centre
Modern complex, with pool, 'Black Hole' flume, wave machine and lots more, Penistone Road, S6 2AN, tel: 0114-231 2233, Open 7 days, Adults £3.20, Juniors £1.90.

Golf
Great golf in Sheffield. Book in advance on the day you want to play. Beauchief, Abbey Lane, tel: 0114-236 7274; Birley, Birley Lane, tel: 0114-264 7262; Tinsley, High Hazels Park, tel: 0114-256 0237.

Tourist Information Centre: 0114-279 5901

SHEFFIELD WEDNESDAY FC

Alive & Kicking
Saturdays 2 - 6pm

Hallam FM 97·4 & 103·4 FM

LEADING PLAYERS IN THE FIELD

Sanderson Electronics PLC is a leading supplier of premier computer solutions, is listed on the London Stock Exchange and employs more than 700 people in 25 office locations throughout the United Kingdom, Australia, New Zealand and East Asia. Sanderson has an extensive portfolio of application software packages which operate on a wide variety of hardware platforms under open system environments such as UNIX and DOS. Sanderson is committed to providing its 4000 customers with reliable products of a high quality and with a high standard of service and support.

1. Manufacturing
2. Solicitors
3. Credit Management
4. Finance and Distribution
5. Supply Chain Management
6. Police
7. Direct Marketing
8. Local Government
9. Airports
10. Insurance
11. Printing Industry
12. Healthcare
13. Computer Based Training
14. Schools and Colleges
15. Hotels
16. Production Monitoring
17. Processing Industry
18. Media and Publishing

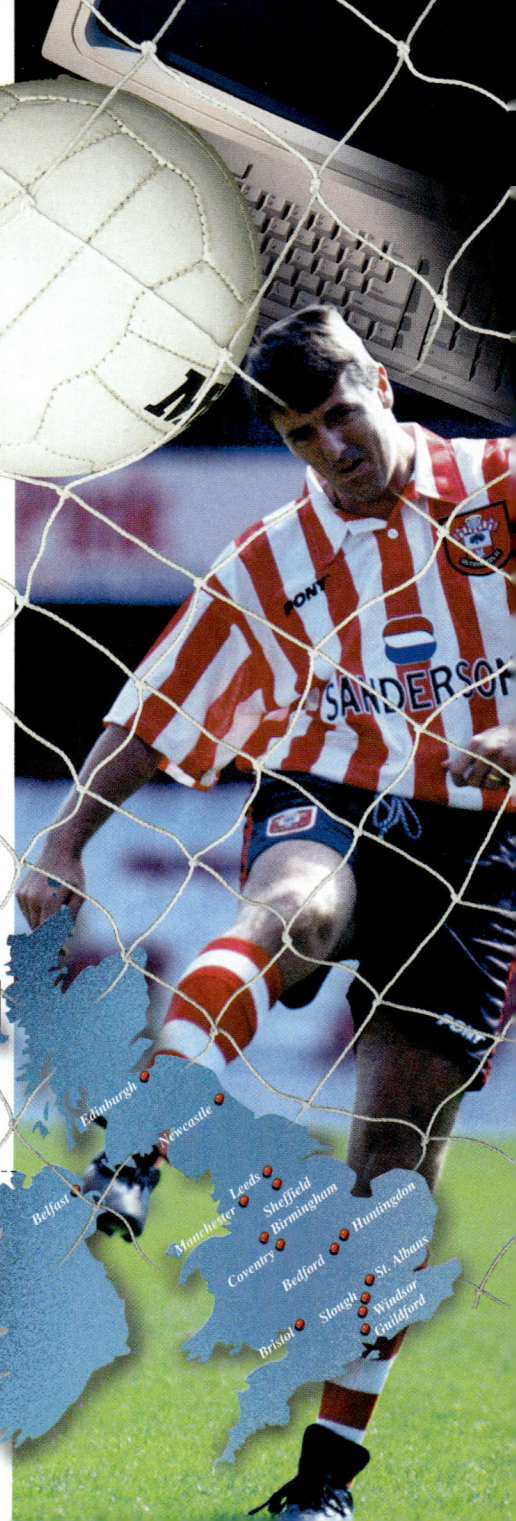

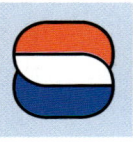

SANDERSON

For Premier Computer Solutions

To obtain further information please tick the relevant box(es) and return a copy of this advertisement with your business card to :-
Sanderson Electronics PLC, Parkway House, Parkway Avenue, Sheffield S9 4WA, or alternatively Telephone (0114) 2827777 or Fax (0114) 2821340

Name _____

Position _____

Address _____

_____

_____

Tel. No. _____

SOUTHAMPTON FC

Club Number: 01703-220 505
Tickets: 01703-337 171
Club Call: 0891-12 11 78
*Calls cost 39p/min. cheap, 49p/min. other times

The Dell
Milton Road
Southampton
SO15 2XH

The Saints Souvenir Shop
The Dell
Mon-Fri: 9.30am - 5pm
Sat. Match Days: 9.30am - 5.30pm
Sun. Match Days: 10am - 2pm
Match Eves: 9.30am - 10.15pm
Tel: 01703-236 400
Fax: 01703-236 300
Mail Order Service:
Tel: 01703-236 400

TICKETS

Booking Information
General Enquiries: 01703-220 505
Recorded Information: 01703-228 575
Credit Card Bookings: 01703-337 171
Ticket Information: 0891-12 15 93*
Ticket Fax Line: 01703-230 882
Travel Club: 01703-334 172

Special Packages
Stadium Tours: 01703-334 172
Corporate Hospitality & Sponsorship Packages:
01703-331 417

Match Day Prices Season 1995/96

	Silver	Gold
Milton Road Stand	£14 (£5)	£17 (£6)
Archers Road Stand	£14 (£5)	£17 (£6)
East Stand		
Upper Tier Centre	£15	£18
Upper Tier Wings	£14	£17
Lower Tier	£12 (£5)	£15 (£6)
West Stand		
Upper Tier Centre	£15	£18
Upper Tier Wings	£14	£17
Lower Tier	£12 (£5)	£15 (£6)

Prices in brackets denote Junior & Sen. Citizen concessions.

STADIUM

Programme £1.50
Official Magazine
Saints Magazine £2
Fanzines
The Ugly Inside £1
Red Stripe £1

MILTON ROAD STAND
Seats 2,897
Ladbrokes
Snack Bar
Toilets

ARCHERS ROAD STAND
Seats 1,299
Snack Bar
Toilets

EAST STAND
Seats 4,882
Snack Bar
Toilets

WEST STAND
Seats 6,074
Ladbrokes
Snack Bar
Toilets

Disabled Access
Milton Road Stand:
12 Wheelchairs, 10 Escorts

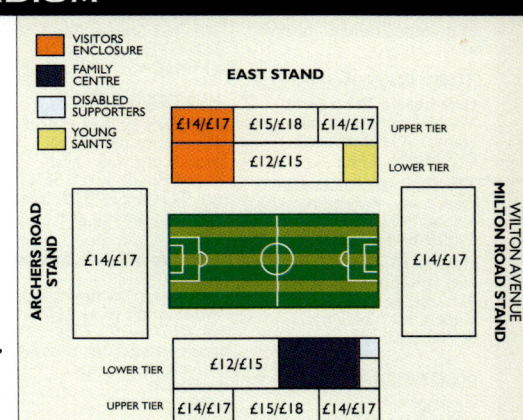

Legend:
- VISITORS ENCLOSURE
- FAMILY CENTRE
- DISABLED SUPPORTERS
- YOUNG SAINTS

EAST STAND
Upper Tier: £14/£17 | £15/£18 | £14/£17
Lower Tier: £12/£15

ARCHERS ROAD STAND: £14/£17

MILTON ROAD STAND (WILTON AVENUE): £14/£17

WEST STAND (HILL LANE/MILTON ROAD)
Lower Tier: £12/£15
Upper Tier: £14/£17 | £15/£18 | £14/£17

SOUTHAMPTON

GETTING TO THE GAME

Southampton play at the Dell, situated half a mile north of the town centre. It is usually possible to park in the streets around the stadium, and there are municipal car parks in the town centre.

BY CAR

From the **North:** Take the M3 to the end and continue onto the The Avenue (A33). Follow for 2½ miles and turn right into Northlands Road. Follow to the end T-junction with Archers Road. The Dell is opposite.

From the **East:** From the M27, exit at Junction 7 to Southampton on the A334. At the first roundabout, take the second exit into Thornhill Park Road (A334), which becomes Bitterne Road (A3024). Continue along for 2 miles, crossing the River Itchen on the Northam Bridge and round onto Charlotte Place roundabout. Take the third exit - Dorset Street (A33) - and continue along for ½ mile. Turn left into Archers Road. The Dell is on the left.

From the **West:** From the M27, exit at Junction 3 onto the M271 southbound. At the roundabout go left into Redbridge Road (A3024). Continue over the next roundabout and then straight for 2 miles, turning left at the junction into Central Station Bridge. At the roundabout turn right into Commercial Road, then first left into Hill Lane. After 0.3 mile turn right at the second set of traffic lights into Archers Road. The Dell is on the right.

BY TRAIN

Southampton Central Railway Station (tel: 01703-229 393) is a ten minute walk to the ground.

BY BUS

From the city centre, either the No.5 or No.25
Bus Information tel: 01703-553 011

IN THE AREA

RADIO
South Coast Radio - Power FM, 103.2 FM; Ocean FM, 96.7 FM & 97.5 FM: Sports bulletins on every station, main sports coverage on Ocean FM Sat 2pm - 6pm.
Radio Solent - 96.1FM, 999MW: Sat 2pm - 6pm, live commentary, interviews, results, phone-in.

TOBY RESTAURANTS
Cowherds Toby Grill
The Avenue, Southampton, Hants. SO1 2NN, tel: 01703-556 344.
TJ's Restaurant & Bar
Peak Lane, Fareham, Hants. PO14 3AA, tel: 01329-844 377.
Happy Cheese
198 Lyndhurst Road, Ashurst, Southampton, Hants. SO4 2AR, tel: 01703-293 232.

RESTAURANTS
Georges
1 St. Michaels Street, SO1 0AB, tel: 01703-223 749, from £10 per head.
Porters
Town Quay Road, SO1 0AR, tel: 01703-221 159, seafood specialities, from £30 per head.
La Margherita
4-6 Commercial Road, SO1 0GE, tel: 01703-333 390, from £12 per head.
Macdonalds
361-363 Shirley Road, SO1 5TD, tel: 01703-511 450

HOTELS / B&B
Hunters Lodge Hotel
15 ensuite rooms, all mod. cons., 25 Landguard Road, SO15 5DL, tel: 01703 227 919, from £30 per person per night.
The Woodlands Lodge Hotel
16 rooms, Bartley Road, Woodlands, SO4 2GN, tel: 01703-292 257, from £49.50 per person per night, incl. full breakfast.
Landguard Lodge
13 rooms, 7 ensuite, 21 Landguard Road, SO15 5DL, tel: 01703-636 904, from £13 per person per night.

PLACES TO VISIT
The Rapids
Giant 70 metre slide, bubble bursts, bubble baths, spa, fitness suite, Southampton Road, Romsey, SO51 8AF, tel: 01794 830 333.
The Waterfront
Quasar, specialty shops, coastal and river cruises, special events all year round, at the Marina, SO1 1JS, tel: 01703-228 353.
Dry Ski for Free
Southampton Ski Centre, Sports Centre, Basset, SO16 7AY, tel: 01703-790 970, Open 7 days, Mon-Fri 9am - 9pm, Sat 9am - 7pm, Sun 10am - 7pm, Adults £6.30/hr, Juniors £4.05/hr, 1 ticket for free if others pay normal charge.
Hall of Aviation
See the legendary Spitfire among many other exhibits, Albert Road North, SO15 1GB, tel: 01736 871 524, Open Tue-Sat 10am - 5pm, Sun 12 - 5pm, Adults £2.50, Juniors £1.50, Conc. £2.
Beaulieu
In the heart of the New Forest, palace house and grounds, abbey and exhibition, shops, restaurants, rides, drives, Brockenhurst, Hants, SO42 7ZN, tel: 01590-612 315 Open daily Easter-Sept 10am - 6pm, Oct-Easter 10am - 5pm, Adults £7.75, Juniors £5.25, Family Ticket £24.

Tourist Information Centre: 01703-553 643

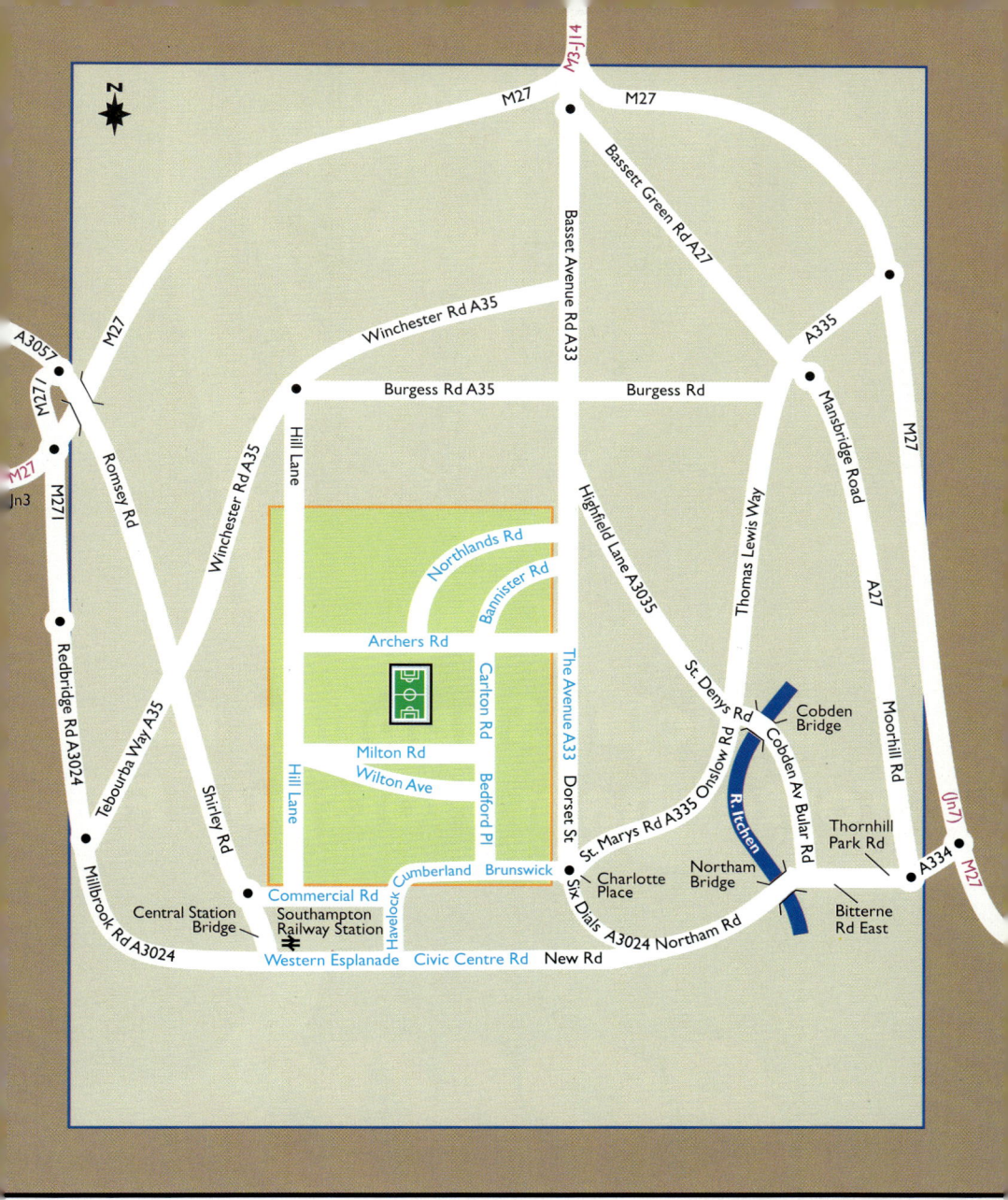

SOUTHAMPTON FC

SouthCoast Radio
1170 & 1557 kHz AM

The station for Southampton soccer.

Official Supplier to Tottenham Hotspur FC

PONY™

TOTTENHAM HOTSPUR FC

Club Number: 0181-365 5000
Tickets: 0181-365 5050
Spurs Line: 0891-33 55 55
Calls cost 39p/min. cheap, 49p/min. other times

THFC SPURS

White Hart Lane
748 High Road
Tottenham
London N17 0AP

West Stand Souvenir Shop
Sat. Match Day: 1pm - kickoff,
half-time & 45 mins after the game
Sun. Match Day: 12pm - kickoff,
half-time & 45 mins after the game
Match Eves: 6pm - kickoff,
half-time & 30 mins after the game
West Stand ticket holders only

Spurs Souvenir Shop
1-3 Park Lane, Tottenham
Mon-Sat: 9.30am - 5.30pm
Sat. Match Days: 9.30am - kickoff,
plus 75 mins after the game
Sun. Match Days: 12pm - kickoff,
plus 45 mins after the game
Match Eves: 9.30am - kickoff,
plus 30 mins after the game
Tel: 0181-365 5042
<u>Mail Order Service:</u>
Tel: 0181-808 5959

Spurs Sportswear Store
766 High Road, Tottenham
Mon-Sat: 9.30am - 5.30pm
Sat. Match Days: 9.30am - kickoff,
plus 75 mins after the game
Sun. Match Days: 12pm - kickoff,
plus 45 mins after the game
Match Eves: 9.30am - kickoff,
plus 30 mins after the game
Tel: 0181-365 5041
<u>Mail Order Service:</u>
Tel: 0181-808 5959

TICKETS

Booking Information
General Enquiries: 0181-365 5050
Spurs Ticket & Competition Line: 0891-33 55 66*
Credit Card Bookings: 0171-396 4567
Travel Club: 0181-365 5100

Special Packages
Stadium Tours: 0181-365 5000
Corporate Hospitality,
Match Sponsorship Packages,
Match Ball and Programme Sponsorship,
106 Executive Boxes and Suites,
Centenary Club, Legends Club, Touchline Club
and Vice Presidents Executive Club,
contact the Commercial Office: 0181-365 5010

Match Day Prices Season 1995/96

	Standard	Premier
North Members Stand		
Upper Tier	£16 (£8)	£19 (£9.50)
Lower Tier	£14 (£7)	£17 (£8.50)
West Stand		
Upper Tier	£27	£32
Lower Tier	£20	£25
East Stand		
Upper Tier Members	£20 (£10)	£23 (£11.50)
Upper Tier Non-Members	£22	£27
Lower Tier Members	£18 (£9)	£21 (£10.50)
Lower Tier Non-Members	£18	£21
South Stand		
Upper Tier	£18	£21
Lower Tier	£15	£18

Prices in brackets denote concessions for Juniors and Senior Citizens

STADIUM

Programme £1.80
<u>Official Magazine</u>
Spurs Monthly £2.00
<u>Fanzines</u>
Spur of the Moment £1.00
Cock a Doodle Doo £1.50

MEMBERS STAND
NORTH
Seats 6,932
Fast Food (with disabled section)
Ladbrokes
Licensed Bar
Toilets
Disabled Toilets

WEST STAND
Seats 6,891
72 Exec. Boxes
Danny Blanchflower Suite
Bill Nicholson Suite
Centenary Club
Touchlines Exec. Club
Fast Food
Licensed Bars
Snack Bars
Toilets
Customer Care Lifts
Disabled Toilets

EAST STAND
Seats 10,860
34 Exec. Suites
Legends Exec. Club
Fast Food
Ladbrokes
Licensed Bars
Snack Bars
Toilets
Customer Care Lift
Police Room
First Aid Room

SOUTH STAND
Seats 8,464
Fast Food
Ladbrokes
Licensed Bars
Snack Bars
Toilets
Customer Care Lift
First Aid Room
Disabled Toilets

VISITORS ENCLOSURE
FAMILY ENCLOSURE
DISABLED ENCLOSURE

WORCESTER AVENUE
EAST STAND
UPPER TIER S:£20/P:£23
LEGENDS
LOWER TIER S:£18/P:£21

PAXTON ROAD
NORTH MEMBERS STAND
UPPER TIER S:£16 P:£19
LOWER TIER S:£14 P:£17
S:£18 £21 (lower)

LOWER TIER S:£20/P:£25
UPPER TIER S:£27/P:£32
PRESS
S:£20/P:£25
WEST STAND
HIGH ROAD
Main Entrance

PARK LANE
SOUTH STAND
LOWER TIER S:£15/P:£18
UPPER TIER S:£18/P:£21
Ticket Office
Away Supporters Entrance

Disabled Access
North & South Stands; 50 Chairs, 1 Helper per person; 4 Stewards, 2 Supervisors, 1 Nurse

Disabled Supporters Entrance
Disabled Supporters Entrance

Getting to the Game

Tottenham Hotspurs' White Hart Lane ground is situated in North London, approx. 6 miles from the city centre. Parking restrictions are extensive around the ground; even more so on match days when there is no entry into Paxton Road and Park Lane two hours before the match and one hour afterwards. There are several private car parks near the ground (£5-£10), and it is advised to arrive early before they fill up. Otherwise, park across town and come in via the underground.

By Car

From the **North:** From the M1, join the M25 heading towards Harlow. Turn right onto the A10 and follow as it becomes Great Cambridge Road. Half a mile past the junction with the North Circular, turn left into White Hart Lane, or continue along and then left into Lordship Lane.

Alternative route from the **North:** From the M1 or A1, join the North Circular Road (A406) eastbound and continue for approx. 7 miles. At Edmonton, at the traffic lights junction with the A1010, turn right into Fore Street. Follow for three quarters of a mile. Spurs is on the left.

From the **South:** From the M23, join the A23 and continue to the junction with the A3. From the A3, cross the Thames over London Bridge, taking the right fork into Bishopsgate (A10). Keep to this straight road for approx. 5½ miles even as it becomes the A1010 after Bruce Grove. Continue along into High Road. Spurs is on the left.

From the **East:** From the A11, join the North Circular Road (A406) westbound and follow for 3½ miles. At the junction with the A1010, turn left into Fore Street. Spurs is on the left.

From the **West:** Take the M4 to Chiswick Roundabout and turn left onto the North Circular Road (A406). Follow the North Circluar eastbound to Edmonton. At the traffic lights junction with the A1010, turn right into Fore Street. Follow for three quarters of a mile. Spurs is on the left.

Alternative route from the **West:** From the M4, continue over Chiswick Roundabout into the A4 and take the M41 to Westway (A40). Follow along into Marylebone Road (A501) and into City Road. At Old Street roundabout, turn left into Old Street, continuing to Kingsland Road (A10). Turn left and continue along the A10 for about 5 miles, keeping straight as it becomes the A1010 after Bruce Grove. Continue along into High Road. Spurs is on the left.

By Train

There are three Underground Stations within walking distance of the stadium: Tottenham Hale and Seven Sisters on the Victoria Line, and Turnpike Lane on the Piccadilly Line. Seven Sisters is also a convenient British Rail station. Two other British Rail stations nearby are White Hart Lane and Bruce Grove.

Kings Cross - Victoria Line to Seven Sisters
Euston - Victoria Line to Seven Sisters
Paddington - Circle or Hammersmith & City Lines to Kings Cross, Victoria Line to Seven Sisters
Victoria - Victoria Line to Seven Sisters
Waterloo - Northern Line to Warren Street, Victoria Line to Seven Sisters

In The Area

Radio
London Radio - 97.3 FM & 1152 AM: 24-hour extensive sports coverage seven days a week, twice an hour - previews, results, reviews.

Radio 5 Live - 909 MW General sports coverage - live commentary on main matches plus regular updated bulletins.

Toby Restaurants
George
5 The Town, Enfield, Middx. EN2 6LE, tel: 0181-363 0074.

Gryphon
Vera Avenue, Grange Park, London N21 1RE, tel: 0181-360 7561

Greengate
Horns Road, Barkingside, Ilford, London IGT2 6BE, tel: 0181-518 6078.

Restaurants
San Marco
Around £13 per head, 1-3 Station Building, Bruce Grove, London N17 6QY, tel: 0181-808 9494

Jashan Tandoori
19 Turnpike Lane, N8 0EP, tel: 0181-340 9880

Pizza Bella
From £8, 4 Park Road, London N8 8TD, tel: 0181-343 8541

Hotels / B&B
Holiday Inn
153 ensuite rooms, bar, restaurant, free parking, Garden Court, Tilling Road, Brent Cross, London NW2 1LP, tel: 0181-455 4777, from £72 per double room, incl. breakfast.

Hospitality Inn Charlotte Hotel
175 rooms, bar, restaurant, mod. facilities, free parking, Bayswater Road, W2 3HL, tel: 0171-262 4461, from £95 per double room.

Kenwood House Hotel
16 rooms, mod. cons., 114 Gloucester Place, WIH 3DB, tel: 0171-935 3473, B&B from £27.

Taxis
Apollo Cars
46 White Hart Lane, N17, tel: 0181-365 1475

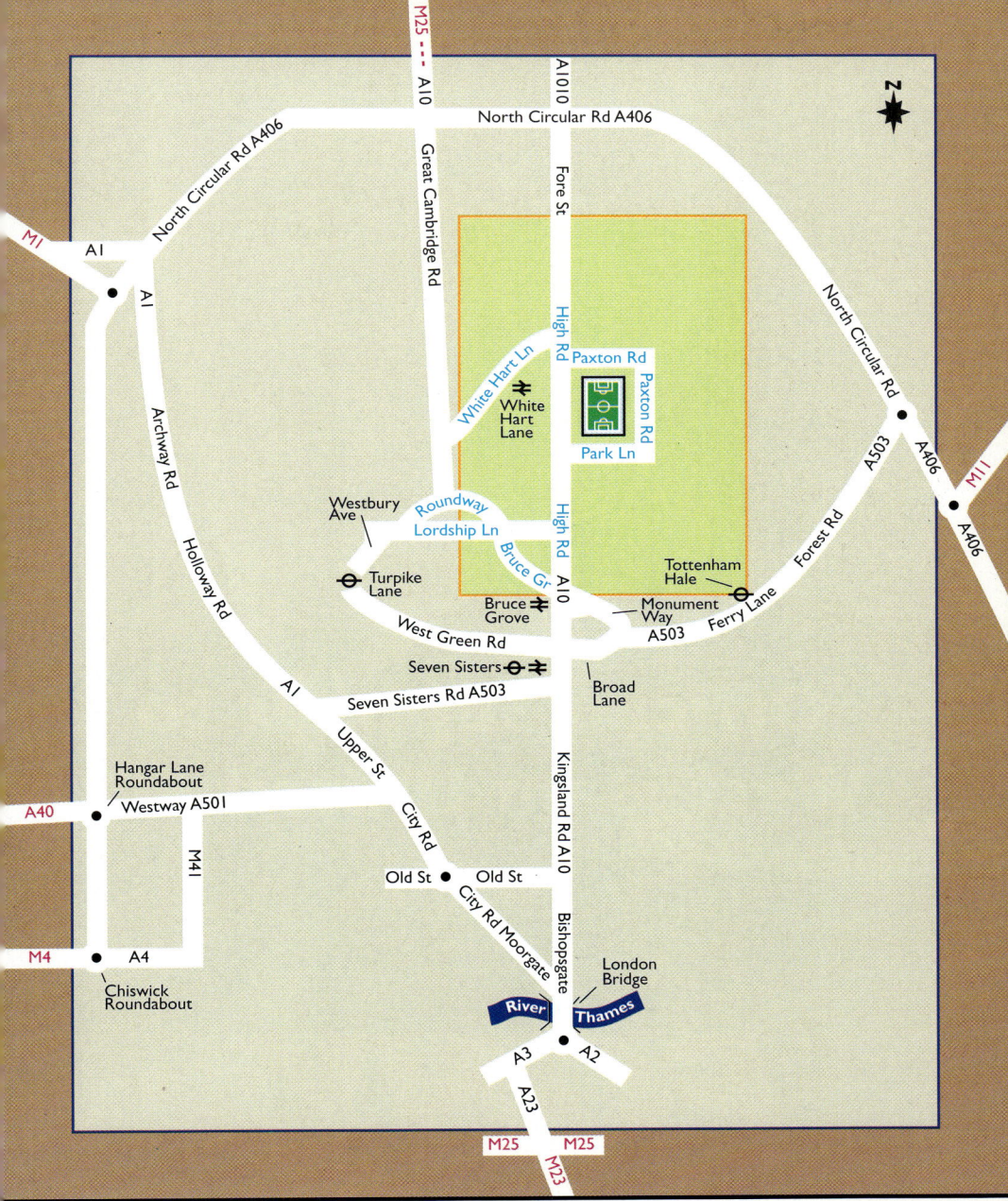

TOTTENHAM HOTSPUR FC

The only sports channel you'll ever need — London news 97.3 fm

Official Supplier to West Ham United FC

PONY™

WEST HAM UNITED FC

Club Number: 0181-548 2748
Tickets: 0181-548 2700
Club Call: 0891-12 11 65
*Calls cost 39p/min. cheap, 49p/min. other times

WHUFC HAMMERS

Boleyn Ground
Green Street
Upton Park
London E13 9AZ

Hammers Merchandise
Boleyn Ground, Upton Park
Mon-Fri: 9.30am - 5pm
Sat./Sun. Match Days: 9.30am - kickoff,
plus 30 mins. after the game
Match Eves: 9.30am - kickoff,
plus 30 mins. after the game
Non-match Sats: 9.30am - 1pm
Tel: 0181-548 2722
Fax: 0181-472 0616
<u>Mail Order Service:</u>
Tel: 0181-548 2730

TICKETS

Booking Information
General Enquiries: 0181-548 2700
Recorded Information: 0181-472 3322
Ticket Info Line: 0891-12 18 65*
Credit Card Bookings: 0181-548 2700
Travel Club: 0181-548 2700

Special Packages
Restaurant Facilities available to Members
Stadium Tours, first Thursday of each month, contact R. Morgan or T. Lewin: 0181-548 2707
Corporate Hospitality & Sponsorship Packages, contact the Promotions Department: 0181-548 2777

Match Day Prices Season 1995/96

	Adult	Juv/Sen.Cit.
West Stand	£17-£25	£10
East Stand Upper Tier	£17-£25	£10
Bobby Moore Stand	£14-£21	£10
Centenary Stand (North)	£15	£8

Reductions are available to members.

STADIUM

Programme £1.50

<u>Official Magazine</u>
Hammers News Monthly £2

<u>Fanzines</u>
On the Terraces £1
On a Mission from God £1
Over Land and Sea £1

WEST STAND
Seats 7,994
Chinese Food
Ladbrokes
Licensed Bar
Refreshment Bars
Toilets

EAST STAND
Seats 4,699
Ladbrokes
Licensed Bar
Refreshment Bars
Toilets

BOBBY MOORE STAND
Seats 7,558
Ladbrokes
Licensed Bar
Mexican Food
Refreshment Bars
Toilets

CENTENARY STAND
Seats 5,646
Chinese Food
Ladbrokes
Licensed Bar
Refreshment Bars
Toilets

Disabled Access
West Stand Lower:
20 Wheelchairs, 24 Helpers;
North Stand:
31 Wheelchairs, 26 Helpers,
Bobby Moore Stand Lower:
36 Wheelchairs, 36 Helpers.

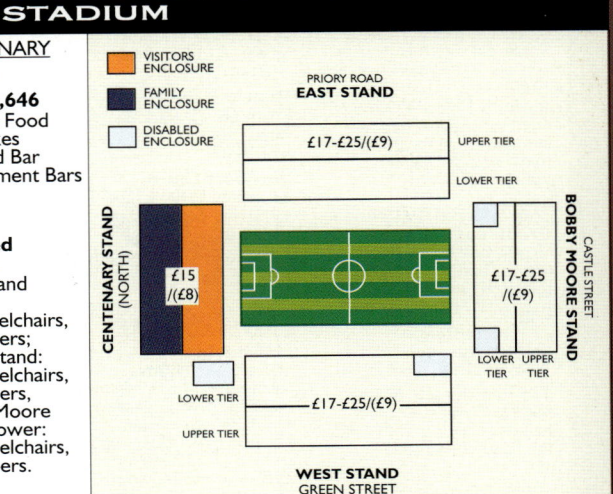

WEST HAM UNITED

GETTING TO THE GAME

West Ham play at Upton Park, in London's East End, approx. 7 miles from London's city centre. There is usually ample parking available in the streets around the ground, but it should be noted that for some matches the police are on hand to direct traffic flow and parking.

BY CAR

From the **North:** From the M1 or A1, join the North Circular (A406) eastbound. Continue for 17 miles until the roundabout junction with the A214 Barking Road. Turn right into Barking Road and continue along for approx. two miles, and turn right at the second traffic lights into Green Street. Upton Park is on the right.

From the **South:** From the M23, join the M25 eastbound to Junction 31, after the Dartford Tunnel. Travel west into London on the A13 for 14 miles, through Rainham and Dagenham. When the A13 becomes Newham Way, turn left at the junction with the A124 into Barking Road. After approx. 1 mile, turn left into Green Street. Upton Park is on the right.

From the **East:** From the M11, exit at Junction 4 onto the North Circular (A406) eastbound for 4 miles. At the roundabout junction with the A214 Barking Road, turn right into Barking Road and continue along for approx. two miles, and turn right at the second traffic lights into Green Street. Upton Park is on the right.

From the **West:** Approaching from either the M4 or the A40, join the North Circular Road (A406) eastbound, and follow all the way around for approx. 27 miles to the junction with the A214 Barking Road. Turn right into Barking Road and continue along for approx. two miles, turning right at the second traffic lights into Green Street. Upton Park is on the right.

BY TRAIN

The nearest Underground Stations are Upton Park and East Ham, both on the District Line.
Kings Cross - Hammersmith & City Line to Whitechapel, District Line to Upton Park
Euston - Northern Line to Embankment, District Line to Upton Park
Paddington - Hammersmith & City Line to Whitechapel, District Line to Upton Park
Victoria - District Line to Upton Park
Waterloo - Northern or Bakerloo Line to Embankment, District Line to Upton Park

IN THE AREA

RADIO
London Radio - 97.3 FM & 1152 AM: 24-hour extensive sports coverage seven days a week, twice an hour - previews, results, reviews.

Radio 5 Live - 909 MW General sports coverage - live commentary on main matches plus regular updated bulletins.

TOBY RESTAURANTS
Crook Log
Crook Log Road, Bexley Heath, London DA6 8EQ, tel: 0181-303 3337.

Eagle
73 Hollybush Road, Snaresbrook, London E11 1OE, tel: 0181-989 7618.

TJ's Restaurant & Bar
Stirling Corner, Arkley, Barnet, London EN5 1HE, tel: 0181-449 9244.

RESTAURANTS
Green Street Cafe
From £4, opposite the stadium, 570 Green Street, E13 9DA, tel: 0181-470 0363.

Bubble Cafe
From £8, 12 Barking Road, E6 1QD, tel: 0181-471 2107.

Sherbert Dabs
31 Water Lane, E15 4NL, tel: 0181-221 0600.

Pizza Hut
1113 High Street North, E6 1HS, tel: 0181-471 5292.

HOTELS / B & B
Holiday Inn
162 ensuite rooms, restaurants, bars, leisure facilities, private garden, 100 Cromwell Road, London SW7 4ER, tel: 0171-373 2222, from £165 per double room.

The Edward Lear Hotel
21 rooms, mod. cons., 30 Seymour Street, London W1H 5WD, tel: 0171-402-5401, from £37.50 per double room, incl. breakfast.

Wigmore Court Hotel
21 rooms, mod. cons., 23 Gloucester Place, London W1H 3PB, tel: 0171-935 0928, from £32 per double room.

PLACES TO VISIT
Camden Lock Market
London's giant thronging Sunday market, arts, crafts, clothes, buskers, Chalk Farm Road, NW1, Camden/Chalk Farm tube, tel: 0171-247 6590, also open Mon-Fri 10-6.

Madame Tussauds
World famous waxworks, Maylebone Road, Baker Street tube, NW1, tel: 0171-935 6861, Open Mon-Fri: 10am - 5pm, Adults £8.25, Conc. £5.25. Combined ticket with Planetarium: Adults £10.25, Conc. £6.55.

Natural History Museum
Dinosaurs, ecology, creepy crawlies, gemstones, human biology, Cromwell Road, SW7, South Kensington tube, tel: 0171-938 9123, Open Mon-Sat: 10am - 5.30pm, Sun: 11am - 5.30pm, Adults £5, Conc. £2.50.

TAXIS
Bell Cars
66 Chingford Mount Road, E4, tel: 0181-527 1066.

Apollo Minicabs
53a Barking Road, E6, tel: 0181-470 1111.

WEST HAM UNITED FC

London news 97.3 fm

...ly sports channel you'll ever need

The of

WIMBLEDON FC

Club Number: 0181-771 2233
Tickets: 0181-771 8841
Club Call: 0891-12 11 75
*Calls cost 39p/min. cheap, 49p/min. other times

WFC DONS

**Selhurst Park
London
SE25 6PY**

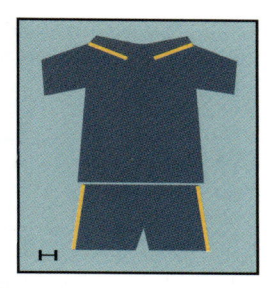

Wimbledon Club Shop
Selhurst Park Stadium
Mon-Fri: 9am - 5.30pm
Sat. Match Days: 9am - kickoff,
plus 45 mins. after the game
Sun. Match Days: 3 hours before kickoff,
plus 30 mins. after the game
Match Eves: 9am - 30 mins. after the game
Tel: 0181-653 5584
Fax: 0181-653 4708

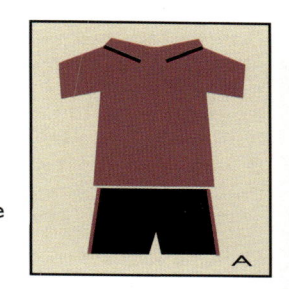

TICKETS

Booking Information
General Enquiries: 0181-771 8841
Credit Card Bookings: 0181-771 8841
Ticket Hotline: 0891-51 61 61*
Travel Club: 0181-771 8841

Special Packages
3 large Restaurants available, ticket-holders only.
You need to book: 0181-653 1876

For children's birthday parties,
contact Tina: 0181-771 2233

Corporate Hospitality & Sponsorship Packages,
contact Sharon Sillitoe: 0181-771 2233

Membership restrictions will be in force at all games.
No membership appications can be processed on
match days.

Match Day Prices Season 1995/96

	Adult	Conc.
Main Stand		
VP's	£40	n/a
Other Areas	£20	£10
Family Enclosure	£10	£5
Arthur Wait Stand	£15	n/a
Holmesdale Road Stand	£10	£5
Whitehorse Lane Stand	£10	£5

Conc: Juveniles/Senior Citizens
CG: For Crazy Gang members, ticket prices are discounted
by £3(Adults)/£2(Conc.) for Main Stand 'Other Areas'; £2/£1
for Main Stand Family Enclosure; £2/£2 Arthur Wait Stand;
£2/£1 Whitehorse Lane and Holmesdale Stands

STADIUM

Programme
£1.50

Fanzines
Go Jo Go
50p
Tenants Extra
50p
Sour Grapes
50p
Hoof the Ball Up
£1
Wandering Hans
£1

MAIN STAND
Seats 6,000
Executive
Lounges & Boxes
Colour T.V.
Fast Food
Ladbrokes
Licensed Bars
Snacks
Restaurants
Toilets

ARTHUR WAIT STAND
Seats 10,000
Ladbrokes
Snacks
Toilets

HOLMESDALE ROAD STAND
Seats 8,000
Colour T.V.
Fast Food
Ladbrokes
Licensed Bars
Snacks
Toilets

WHITEHORSE LANE STAND
Seats 2,245
Hospitality
Boxes
Snacks
Toilets

Disabled Access
Park Road,
Arthur Wait
Stand,
28 Wheelchairs,
1 Helper per
person
Headphone
commentary
available for 12
blind/partially
sighted.

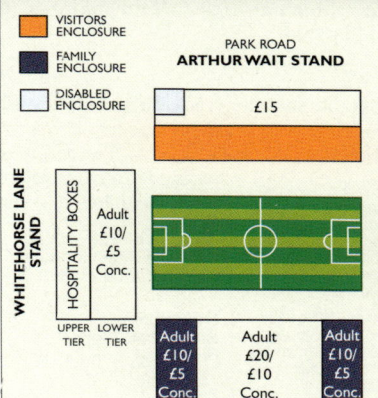

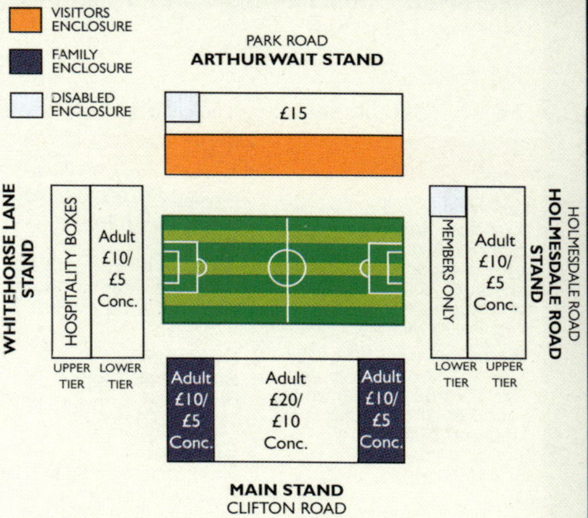

VISITORS ENCLOSURE
FAMILY ENCLOSURE
DISABLED ENCLOSURE

PARK ROAD
ARTHUR WAIT STAND
£15

WHITEHORSE LANE STAND
HOSPITALITY BOXES
Adult £10/ £5 Conc. (UPPER TIER / LOWER TIER)

Adult £20/ £10 Conc.
Adult £10/ £5 Conc.

MEMBERS ONLY
Adult £10/ £5 Conc. (LOWER TIER / UPPER TIER)
HOLMESDALE ROAD STAND

MAIN STAND
CLIFTON ROAD

GETTING TO THE GAME

Wimbledon play at Selhurst Park in South London, nine miles from the city centre. Parking is allowed in most of the neighbourhood streets and it is usually possible to leave the car quite close to the stadium. However, on match days Holmesdale Road and Park Road adjacent to the ground are closed to vehicular traffic. Also, when a capacity crowd or all ticket match is anticipated all roads surrounding the stadium are closed to pedestrian traffic unless tickets are produced at the barriers.

BY CAR

From the **North:** From the M1, continue to the end of the motorway and turn right onto the A406 North Circular. From the M40, continue straight along the A40 past Uxbridge to the end and turn right onto the A406 North Circular.
Keep on the North Circular until Chiswick Roundabout, then take the A205 South Circular Kew Road, which joins the A3 to Wandsworth. Turn right onto Trinity Road (A214), through Tooting Bec to Streatham. Turn right onto Streatham High Road (A23). After 1 mile turn left into Green Lane (B273). This becomes Parchmore Road. At the end, turn left into High Street and along into Whitehorse Lane. Selhurst Park is on the right.

From the **South:** Approaching from either the M25 or the M23, leave at Junction 7 for the A23. After 3 miles, turn right into Bridgstock Road (B266), which is where the A23 meets the A235. Continue along this road as it becomes High Street, crossing over Grange Road and straight into Whitehorse Lane. Selhurst Park is on the right.

From the **East:** Leave the M25 at Junction 4 for the A21. This will lead to Glebe Road (A232). Follow Glebe Road and you will see signs for Croydon. Turn right onto Shirley Road (A215), signposted Norwood, and follow along around the Addiscombe Road dog-leg into Spring Lane. After about 2 miles, turn left into White Horse Lane. Selhurst Park is on the left.

From the **West:** Take the M4 to Chiswick Roundabout. Then same as from the North.

From other points within **London** north of the river: Make your way to the most convenient bridge over the Thames and follow the directions on the map.

BY TRAIN

There are two British Rail stations nearby: Selhurst and Norwood. Both are about five minutes walking distance from Selhurst Park. Trains run regularly from Victoria.
Kings Cross - Victoria Line to Victoria, BR to Selhurst, Norwood Junction.
Euston - Northern Line to Warren Street, Victoria Line to Victoria, BR to Selhurst, Norwood Junction.
Paddington - Circle Line to Victoria, BR to Selhurst, Norwood Junction.
Charing Cross - Northern Line to Embankment, Circle & District Line to Victoria, BR to Selhurst, Norwood Junction.
Waterloo - Norther Line to Embankment, Circle & District Line to Victoria, BR to Selhurst, Norwood Junction.

BY BUS

68[A] to Whitehorse Lane, **157, 75** to Selhurst Road

IN THE AREA

RADIO
London Radio - 97.3 FM & 1152 AM: 24-hour extensive sports coverage seven days a week, twice an hour - previews, results, reviews.

Radio 5 Live - 909 MW General sports coverage - live commentary on main matches plus regular updated bulletins.

TOBY RESTAURANTS
Eden Park Toby Carving Room
422 Upper Elmers End Road, Beckenham, Kent BR3 3HQ, tel: 0181-650 2233.

Beulah Spa
Beulah Hill, Upper Norwood, London SE19 3DS, tel: 0181-653 2051.

Cardinal
23 Francis Street, Westminster, London SW1P 1DN, tel: 0171-834 7260.

RESTAURANTS
T.G.I. Friday's
702/704 Purley Way, SE19, tel: 0181-681 1313.

Penge Tandoori
53 Penge Road, SE25, tel: 0181-776 6428.

HOTELS
Holiday Inn
153 ensuite rooms, bar, restaurant, free parking, Garden Court, Tilling Road, Brent Cross, London NW2 1LP, tel: 0181-455 4777, from £72 per double room, incl. breakfast.

TAXIS
Area Cars
122[A] Whitehorse Lane, SE25, 0181-771 5335

Admiral 5 Star Cars
174 North End Road, SE25, tel: 0181-681 8700.

WIMBLEDON FC

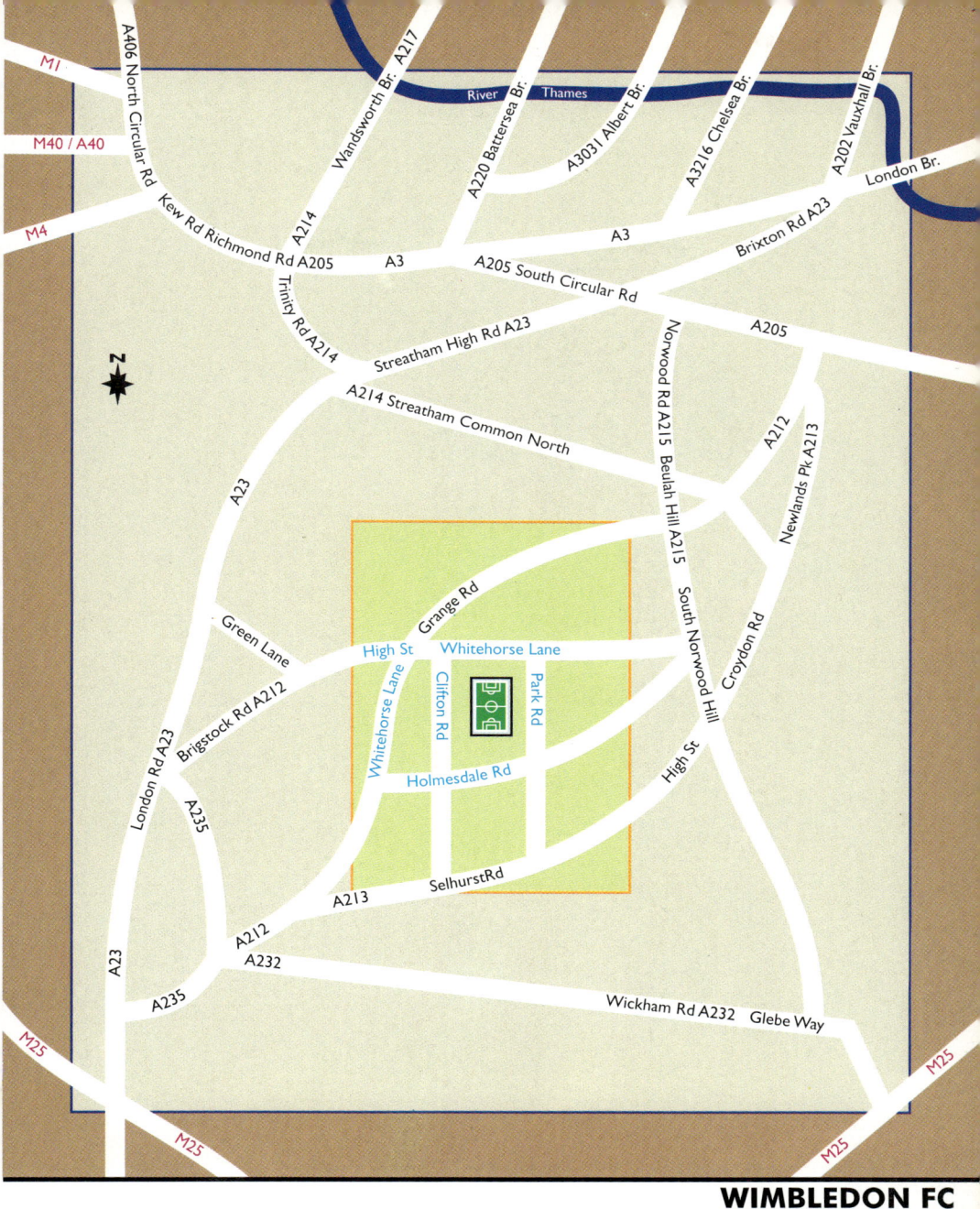

The only sports channel you'll ever need — London news 97.3 fm

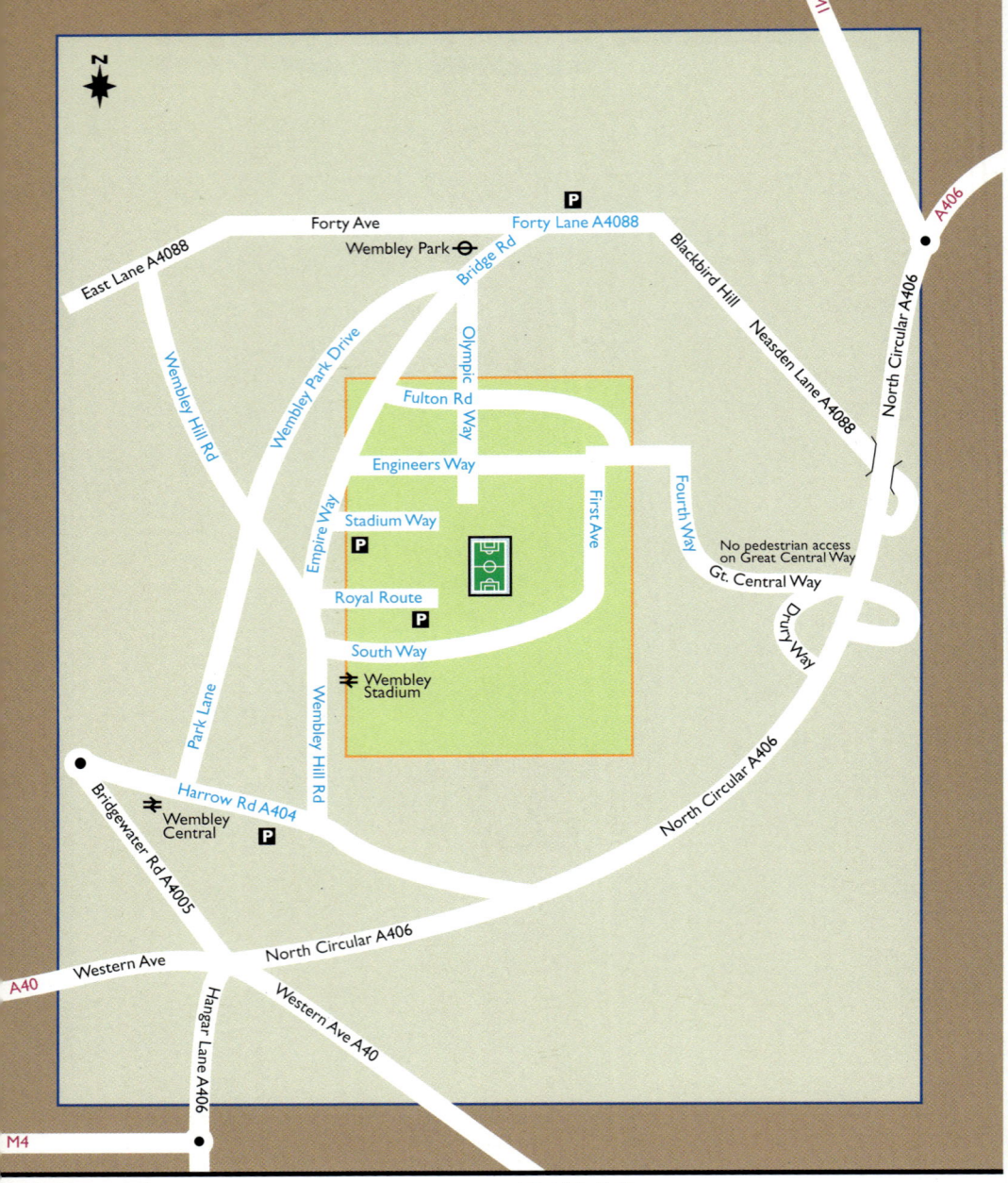

Underground
Wembley Park Station (Metropolitan Line) is five mins. walk from the Stadium, with services from Baker Street, Kings Cross and Liverpool Street stations.
Wembley Central Station (Bakerloo Line) is ten mins. walk from the Stadium, with services from Elephant & Castle, Charing Cross, Baker Street and Marylebone Stations.
For full details, tel: 0171-222 1234

Bus
The 18, 83, 92, 182 and 192 services all pass close by the Wembley Complex.

British Rail
Wembley Stadium Station is next door to the Complex, Marylebone to Banbury service on the Chiltern Line. It may be convenient to park at one of the stations close to the M40, in particular: Bicester North, High Wycombe, Beaconsfield and Banbury.
For full details, tel: 0171-262 6767 or 01494-441 561.
Wembley Central Station is ten mins. walk to the Stadium, Euston to Watford service and Euston to Milton Keynes and Northampton services.
For full details, tel: 01923-245 001